Ignatius of Antioch

—————————— & ——————————

Polycarp of Smyrna

A New Translation
and
Theological Commentary

Revised and Expanded Edition

Kenneth J. Howell

Early Christian Fathers Series: 1

CHResources

CHResources

P.O. Box 8290

Zanesville, OH 43702

740-450-1175

CHResources is a registered trademark of

The Coming Home Network International

13 12 11 10 09   1 2 3 4 5

The material on Ignatius of Antioch was previously published
under the title *Ignatius of Antioch A New Translation and Theological
Commentary* (Zanesville OH: *CHResources*, 2008)

ISBN 978-0-9800066-5-0

Library of Congress Cataloging-in-Publication Data

Ignatius, Saint, Bishop of Antioch, d. ca. 110.

[Correspondence. English]

Ignatius of Antioch & Polycarp of Smyrna : a new translation and
theological commentary / Kenneth J. Howell. – Rev. and expanded ed.

    p. cm. – (Early Christian Fathers series ; 1)

Includes bibliographical references and indexes.

ISBN 978-0-9800066-5-0 (alk. paper)

    1. Ignatius, Saint, Bishop of Antioch, d. ca. 110–Correspondence.
2. Apostolic Fathers–Correspondence. 3. Theology–History–Early
church, ca. 30-600. 4. Polycarp, Saint, Bishop of Smyrna. I. Title. II.
Title: Ignatius of Antioch and Polycarp of Smyrna. III. Series.

BR65.I3E5 2009

270.1092'2–dc22

                                    2009036110

Cover Design by Jennifer Bitler www.doxologydesign.com

Book layout by Mary Clare Piecynski

*Ad redintegrationem unitatis
omnium Christianorum dedicatum*

Table of Contents

Preface

To the attentive reader of early Christian writings, the names of St. Ignatius of Antioch and St. Polycarp of Smyrna stand as powerful witnesses to the life of the church in the second century. Outside the canon of the New Testament few leaders of the early church have given us so much clarity about the life of Christians of that period. A man who probably knew some of the apostles themselves, Ignatius became the second or third bishop of Antioch in Syria. Martyred in Rome some time during the reign of the emperor Trajan (98-117), Ignatius's seven authentic letters give us snapshots of the faith and life of the churches of Asia Minor in a manner that is equaled only by the *Acts of the Apostles* and the seven letters of the *Apocalypse*. More is known about the life and martyrdom of Polycarp but fewer of his letters have survived antiquity. Polycarp, the bishop of Smyrna, was martyred around the mid-second century. Ignatius passed through Smyrna around 110 en route to Rome. Together, they give us unique insights into the theology, church practice, and hope of early Christians.

St. Ignatius has been celebrated and his letters studied with great diligence for centuries. Yet, despite numerous translations into modern languages, commentators on Ignatius have not always understood the broader and deeper theology that underlies his writings. Like St Paul's letters in the New

Testament, Ignatius's epistles were "occasional writings" (*Gelegenheitschriften*) penned while en route to Rome. They are not anything like the systematic treatises of theology that we find later in the second century (e.g. Irenaeus of Lyons, *Against Heresies*) but they are examples of the high regard the ancients had for writing exemplary instructional epistles. Behind and within these letters, however, lies a profound theology that was to become seminal for later Christian thinkers. In Ignatius's writings we stand at the source of a long tradition that still shapes Christianity today in both the East and the West. The translations and commentary contained in this book are designed to lay bare that Ignatian theology.

Ignatius has endured the vicissitudes of centuries of scholarship. At one extreme, there is the naive acceptance of writings ascribed to him (in the so-called long recension, e.g. *Letter to Mary*) which scholars now universally agree are not authentically his. The other is an atomistic hyper-historicism that makes Ignatius not only of questionable relevance today but even irrelevant to understanding the wider spectrum of Christian belief and practice of his own time. Professional scholars of early Christianity show a marked tendency to treat each of the earliest Fathers as individuals whose theology was not necessarily shared by others of that time. This, of course, is somewhat difficult to discern in the case of Ignatius because there are so few of his strict contemporaries available to us. The *Didache* and the *Letter to the Philippians* by Polycarp are some of the closest witnesses we have to the time of Ignatius.

Polycarp, like Ignatius, can boast a long history of study by scholars and general readers of early Christianity. However, the only document surviving from his pen, his *Letter to the Philippians*, does not display the theological profundity of Ignatius's letters. Consequently, many scholars have found his work less interesting and worthy of attention. This is a hasty judgment in my estimation. While his only letter bears the marks of pastoral concern rather than theological acumen, it draws on the rich fount of Paul's theology in the New Testament, as Kenneth Berding as recently shown. We may also be justified in making some inferences about Polycarp's teachings from the *Martyrdom of Polycarp*, a document dating most probably from the early third century. This account of the death of the bishop of Smyrna still today ranks as one of the most moving and inspiring martyrologies from the second century.

Every student of the early church fathers, like any scholar doing historical research, must necessarily bring certain presuppositions to the study. Often there is an implicit community of readers that each scholar is addressing, which tends control his interpretations. I am, of course, no different. I have chosen to emphasize the affinities between Ignatius and Polycarp on the one hand, and the writings of the New Testament on the other. The theology of Paul, the most important writer in the canonical New Testament, looms large. We will see that there is a natural and almost expected development from the early catholicity of the later writings in the New Testament (e.g. the Pastorals) to these bishop-martyrs. While most available editions of Ignatius and Polycarp cite passages from the New Testament which they allude to or quote, many current translators have not explored those connections as deeply as one might.

A commentary should above all else explain the text in terms a modern reader can understand. This is a much more challenging task than appears at first. Through many years of teaching I have learned that few readers really plumb the depths of the patristic writings, even those that seem straightforward. Like St. Paul in the New Testament, there is much more to Ignatius and Polycarp than meets the eye. In many aspects of their thought, but especially in their fervent longing for martyrdom, Ignatius and Polycarp seem like men from a different and distant world. I have taken it as my task not only to make these men understandable to the modern reader but even more to engender a desire to be like them. For me, Ignatius and Polycarp are not simply objects of scholarly inquiry. For me, they are Saints, men in whom the desire for martyrdom represents the most profound expression of love for Jesus Christ. This love for Christ explains their pastoral solicitude, their love of the Eucharist, and their concern for unity within the churches. They are not only authors to be read; they are men with whom one can converse. I invite the reader into this conversation with the hope that it will engender that same love of Jesus Christ and the church that so burned in the souls of Ignatius and of Polycarp.

Kenneth J. Howell
17 October 2009, the Memorial of St. Ignatius of Antioch

Note on Text and Translation

Translations from one language to another inevitably involve interpretation. So-called literal translations are impossible and so a translator of ancient Greek must often choose between a more or less literal translation. A more literal translation retains the structure of the original Greek as much as possible and does not attempt to solve interpretative difficulties for the reader. A less literal one aims at readability for the modern reader but sometimes requires interpretative decisions that may also be resolved in a different manner. I have attempted to walk a thin line between these two, sometimes emphasizing readability and at others literalness. I have generally reserved my interpretative decisions for the commentary in the footnotes.

The reader will observe that I have interacted with other English translations in my commentary, especially two recent ones by Bart D. Ehrman and Michael W. Holmes. Both are excellent renderings of the original Greek and deserve close consideration by anyone who undertakes the task. Neither translator has provided a commentary but both rely on certain earlier traditions of translation with which at times I disagree. These disagreements are of two kinds. The first has to do with alternative readings of the Greek text where there is room for legitimate difference of opinion. The second and more debatable has to do with theological issues that may be influenced by the translator's assumptions. No conscientious translator seeks to impose his own views on the original writer but interpretation always requires some assumptions about the writer's meaning. If two translators do not share assumptions, they may disagree about how to translate a given word or phrase. Assumptions can be of many kinds: historical, linguistic, contextual, conceptual, and theological. The last kind shows up in my differences with Ehrman and Holmes at several places. My translations have also been informed by the fine work of P.Th. Camelot O.P. (French) and Walter Bauer (German).

The reader will note that occasionally certain words are placed in brackets [...] in the translation (e.g. see Eph 11:2 and 12:2). This means that the bracketed words are not found in the original Greek text at this point but are strongly implied. Some past translators have simply added such words without indicating their absence in the original. I wanted the reader to know when certain words with heavy content were added by me. The Greek text that provided the basis of this translation is found that in the *Sources chrétiennes* edition (vol 10) of Ignatius's seven letters edited by P.Th. Camelot. In the case of Polycarp's *Letter to the Philippians*, I used the Greek text in Bihlmeyer and Schneemelcher *Die apostolischen Väter*, 3rd ed. (1970). For the *Martyrdom of Polycarp* I used Herbert Musurillo, *The Acts of the Christian Martyrs*. (Oxford: Clarendon Press, 1972). These editions all appear in the online resource *Thesaurus Linguae Graecae*. When significant variations occurred in manuscripts not chosen by these editors, I have noted them in the footnotes.

Abbreviations

References to biblical books will follow standard abbreviations in American English.

Abbreviations for Ignatius's letters and parts within them:

Eph = Ignatius's *Letter to the Ephesians* (references to Paul's Letter to the Ephesians will be made clear in the context).

Magn = Ignatius's *Letter to the Magnesians.*

Philad = Ignatius's *Letter to the Philadelphians.*

Polyc = Ignatius's *Letter to Polycarp.*

Rom = Ignatius's *Letter to the Romans* (references to Paul's Letter to the Romans will be made clear in the context).

Smyrn = Ignatius's *Letter to the Smyrneans.*

Trall = Ignatius's *Letter to the Trallians*

Sal = Salutation

Abbreviations of works about or by Polycarp:

Mart Polyc = *Martyrdom of Polycarp*

Phil Polyc = Polycarp's *Letter to the Philippians*

Other Abbreviations:

BAG = *A Lexicon of the New Testament and Other Early Christian Literature* (Chicago: University of Chicago Press, 4th ed. 1952)

Bauer = Bauer, Walter, and Henning Paulsen *Die Briefe des Ignatius von Antiochia und der Polykarpbrief* (1985)

Camelot = Camelot, P. T. *Ignace d'Antioche. Polycarpe de Smyrne. Lettres. Martyre de Polycarpe,* (1969).

Ehrman = *The Apostolic Fathers* edited and translated by Bart Ehrman (2003)

Holmes = *The Apostolic Fathers: The Apostolic Fathers Greek Texts,* and *English Translations* 3rd ed. Edited and translated by Michael W. Holmes (2007).

Lampe = *A Greek Patristic Lexicon* edited by G.W.H. Lampe (1961)

LS = *A Greek-English Lexicon* compiled by Henry George Liddell and Robert Scott with a 1968 supplement (Oxford: Oxford at the Clarendon Press, 1976 reprint)

Lit = Literal or literally.

LXX = the Septuagint, the Greek translation of the Old Testament around 250 B.C.

MSS = manuscripts

Schoedel = Schoedel, William R. *Ignatius of Antioch A Critical and Historical Commentary on the Seven Letters.* (1985)

Introductory Essays

Chapter One
Who Was Ignatius?

St. Ignatius of Antioch was one of the most important church fathers in the first decades of the church immediately following the apostles. Martyred in Rome some time during the reign of the emperor Trajan (98-117), Ignatius left us seven authentic letters in which he expressed the fundamental ideas of Christianity which still shape the life of the church to this day. These letters reveal a man intent on church unity, animated by a love for Christ, bold in his witness (*marturion*) for the gospel, and humble in his self-evaluation.

Ignatius of Antioch is remembered and loved by Christians today across diverse communions. In the ancient church, Ignatius was quoted and honored by Greek-speaking Christians for his deep faith and the power of his intercession. Even among those Christians who probably had little or no contact with his writings, such as in North Africa, his doctrines of church unity and hierarchy, his profound respect for the liturgy and Eucharist, and his pastoral love for the members of the universal church became the common patrimony of the East and the West.

Ignatius in the Judgment of History

Ignatius is mentioned in many ancient writings.[1] One of the most important comes from Eusebius of Caesarea, the early fourth century church historian, whose *Ecclesiastical History* relates some simple facts about Ignatius.[2] We learn from this source that Ignatius succeeded Peter as the second bishop of Antioch though Eusebius gives no date for that transition. After Ignatius was martyred in Rome, Hero (*heros*) succeeded him as the bishop of Antioch. Eusebius recounts the story of Ignatius's journey to Rome by way of Smyrna and Troas as if it were a reliable tradition that had been handed down. From this we learn that Ignatius wrote four of his seven letters at Smyrna (Ephesians, Magnesia, Tralles, and Romans) while from Troas he wrote two others to churches (Philadelphia and Smyrna) and a more personal one to Polycarp, the bishop of Smyrna. Apparently, both Ignatius and Polycarp had been disciples of the Apostle John.

Polycarp himself had mentioned Ignatius in his own *Letter to the Philippians*. Others prior to Eusebius had spoken of Ignatius as well. Irenaeus mentioned both his martyrdom and his letters in the last half of the second century.[3] As might be expected, we find an enduring tradition of celebration of Ignatius's life in Antioch itself as indicated by a homily of St. John Chrysostom in the late fourth century.[4]

---

1 For references to Ignatius in ancient writings see J.B. Lightfoot, *The Apostolic Fathers: Clement, Ignatius, Polycarp* (Peabody, MA: Hendrickson reprint, 1989) vol. 1 pp. 135-232.

2 Eusebius *Ecclesiastical History* bk 3 ch 36 sec 4ff.

3 Irenaeus *Against Heresies* bk 5 ch 28 sec 4.

4 John Chrysostom *Homily on Saint Ignatius* Patrologia Graeca vol. 50 Col 587-596 (Paris: Migne, 1857-1866).

During the early modern era in which the Protestant and Catholic Reformations took place (16th and 17th centuries), Ignatius became something of a controversial figure primarily because his letters present clear indications of how early Catholic ideas formed in the church. Some Protestant scholars questioned the dates of the Ignatian letters and in fact argued that they date from a much later period of Christian history.[5] The nineteenth century witnessed extensive investigations into the Ignatian letters when some new discoveries of manuscripts raised more questions of dating and authorship. The general conclusion arrived at by a variety of scholars toward the end of that century was that the so-called middle recension was in all probability written by Ignatius himself just as Eusebius had recounted it.[6] That judgment largely continues down to this day. With these seven epistles we may be reasonably certain that we are dealing with the authentic views of the bishop of Antioch in the late first and early second century.

Ignatius's Self Representation

To understand Ignatius's letters, however, we must take into account more than the witness of other writers. We can and should look at how the bishop of Antioch portrays himself.

---

5   See Bart Ehrman's discussion in *The Apostolic Fathers* (Cambridge, MA: Harvard University Press, 2003) pp. 203-213.

6   The Ignatian corpus comes down to us in three recensions, or collections of manuscripts representing different channels of transmission. The middle recension contains the seven letters translated here. The long recension contains other letters and writings ascribed to Ignatius which are almost certainly not his. The short recension is a truncated form of the letters in Syriac that was not known until the mid-nineteenth century.

Perhaps Ignatius's most revelatory references to himself have to do with his being a disciple.[7] Most striking are his assertions that he is just "beginning to be a disciple" if he can undergo martyrdom in Rome because the true disciple is the one who willingly shares in the passion (*pathos*) of Jesus Christ. In one sense, Ignatius is already a disciple but to the Romans he insisted that he will only be a true disciple when the beasts have become his tomb and the world no longer sees his body (Rom 4:2). In Romans 5, Ignatius sees himself as becoming a disciple precisely by the injustices he suffers. Full discipleship will only be achieved by reaching Jesus Christ.[8]

Discipleship defines Ignatius's view of his relationship to Christ. The word "servant" signals best what he thinks of his relationship with the church. Although he is aware of his status as a bishop, he prefers to include himself among the deacons. While he employs two words which can mean "servant" — *doulos* and *diakonos* — he does not use them interchangeably. Ignatius uses *diakonos* as a technical term for the office of deacon while he uses *doulos* to mean "slave." Ignatius uses the latter word in its baser sense in Rom 4:3 where *doulos* parallels "criminal" (*katakritos*) and contrasts with being free. When he speaks about the three ministries of bishop, presbyter, and deacon, he almost always calls the last order "his fellow servants" (*sundouloi*).[9] Particularly revealing is his endearing description of the deacons in the

---

7 The noun *mathetes* ("disciple") or the verb *matheuo* ("be a disciple or learn") occurs 14 times in the Ignatian letters. Those which refer to Ignatius himself are Eph 1:2; 3:1; Trall 5:2; Rom 4:2; 5:1-3; Polyc 7:1.

8 Rom 5:3, "Now I am beginning to be a disciple. Nothing visible or invisible will prevent me from reaching Jesus Christ."

9 See Eph 2:1; Mag 2:1; Trall 4:1; Smyrn 12:2.

Letter to the Magnesians:

> So, since I have seen the entire congregation in the afore-
> mentioned persons, I exhort you to be diligent to practice
> everything in harmony with God, as the bishop leads in the
> place of God and the presbyters in the place of the council
> of the apostles and of the deacons — those sweetest to me[10]
> — who have been entrusted with the service of Jesus Christ
> who was with the Father before all ages and has appeared at
> the end [of the world] (Mag 6:1).

Here Ignatius clearly aligns himself with the deacons
because their office, though under the leadership of bishop
and presbyter, embodies the ideal of Christ by being servants of
the people of God. Why would Ignatius so rarely refer to his
office of bishop and so frequently class himself with the deacons of the church? Like many after him, Ignatius appeals to
the faithful of the church, not on the basis of his rightful
authority — that is assumed — but on the basis of his love for
being the lowliest of its members. Like St. Gregory the Great
centuries later, Ignatius thinks of himself as a servant of the
servants of God. His greatest authority lies in his humility. His
greatest act of service lies in his martyrdom.

Ignatius's Fight Against Heresy and Schism: Docetism

Ignatius was also a valiant warrior in the fight against heresy
and schism. Heresy is a sin against truth; schism is a sin against love.
Knowing that either of these contagions could destroy the church,
Ignatius urged the Christians of Asia Minor to give in to neither.
To understand the vigor of Ignatius's battle, we must know some-

---

10 Camelot and Ehrman translate *glukutaton* as "dear to me," but *glukus* has a basic
meaning of "sweet."

thing of the intellectual culture in which he lived. Scholars have written extensively about this background and offered differing interpretations of the Christianity of the early second century.

Docetism was one of the leading heresies that Ignatius, John the Apostle, and other writers had to face. Before Ignatius, we hear echos of Docetism in the *First Letter of John:*

> Beloved, do not believe every spirit but test the spirits to see if they are of God because many false prophets have gone into the world. By this you know the Spirit of God: every spirit which confesses that Jesus Christ has come in the flesh is from God. And every spirit which does not confess Jesus is not of God. This is the spirit of the antichrist which you have heard is coming and is even now in the world (1 Jn 4:1-3).

John's use of the term "antichrist" must not be read with modern Christian eyes which see the Antichrist as one who is against Christ. The word *anti* can, of course, means "against" in ancient Greek, but it can also mean "instead of." The latter is perhaps the more fundamental meaning because all heresy attempts to substitute a false doctrine for a true one. To substitute a Jesus who was not fully human was the essence of Docetism.[11]

If John wrote his short epistle in the 90s of the first century, say during Domitian's reign, the presence of Docetism behind his letter gives strong evidence that Ignatius's concerns were realistic. We see clear evidence of Ignatius's fight in the *Letter to the Trallians:*

> Now if some who are without God, that is unbelievers, claim he only seemed to have suffered — they are ones for whom the language of appearance is appropriate — then why am I a

---

11 This belief was also the essence of a full-blown Gnosticism later in the second century which Irenaeus attempted to fight in *Against Heresies.*

prisoner and why do I desire to fight with beasts? If it were true,
there is no point to my death. I would be bearing false witness
against the Lord (Trall 10:1).

Ignatius's choice of "only seemed to have suffered" is not a passing comment. It is probably a quotation from his docetic oppo-
nents. Like those in the community to which John wrote who
denied that Jesus had come in the flesh, those Ignatius writes
about deny the physical suffering of Jesus. Ignatius's insistence
on the concrete, earthly, physical reality of the life of Jesus
Christ explains why he speaks of Christ's birth, baptism, death,
and resurrection in real historical terms (see e.g. Eph 7:2; 18:2;
Mag 11:1; Philad 9:2).

Ignatius's fight against Docetism becomes all the clearer in
the *Letter to the Smyrneans*. Almost half of the letter (chaps. 1-7)
in some way refers to the heresy of Docetism. The Docetists
deny the full humanity of Jesus as descended from the line of
David (1:1); they deny his suffering (2:1); they deny the physical
resurrection (3:1); their beliefs deny the authority of the Old
Testament (5:2); they do not believe in the blood of Christ
(6:1); their heterodox teachings deny God's grace and love for
the poor (6:2); and they abstain (*apecho*) from the Eucharist
and prayer with the church because they deny the human presence of Christ in the sacrament (7:1).

Why does Ignatius stress the real humanity of Christ as
John does in 1 Jn 1:1-4? Because everything in the Christian
faith depends on the Incarnation. The Docetists were consistent. Since they denied a real Incarnation and the subsequent
sufferings of Christ, they also denied the human presence of
Christ in the Eucharist. Ignatius accurately perceived that the
denial of the real human life, death, and resurrection of

Christ lies at the root of all sacramental disorder. If God did not become a true man, then salvation is lost, as Athanasius would argue later in the fourth century. And if God did not become man, then he could not communicate his divinity through an assumed humanity in the Eucharist. The denial of such a sacramental world view naturally leads to the rejection of proper obedience to the clergy of the church. As the Eucharist is the ongoing Incarnation of Christ in the world, so the hierarchy of the church established by Christ is the ongoing pastoral care of Christ in the world. This explains two things. One is Ignatius's insistence on obedience to the bishop's authority; the second is that the unity of Christians, or the lack of it, is bound up with obedience to rightful church authority and sacramental truth. The denial of a real Incarnation lies at the heart of the ecumenical problem today as much as it did in Ignatius's day.

In these seven short letters, comprising some 8,000 words, the bishop of Antioch has left the church a venerable heritage of integrated theology. He speaks with authority and humility, with power and with meekness. Above all, his life, ministry, and service to the church were crowned by a martyr's death. Like the apostles before him, St. Ignatius continues to provide an indispensable foundation for all Christendom.

Chapter Two
The Martyrdom of Ignatius

S t. Ignatius was martyred in Rome some time during the reign of the emperor Trajan (A.D. 98-117). From his letters we can infer a sequence of events as follows. He must have faced a trial in Antioch which ended in his being sent off to Rome, either to stand trial before the emperor or to be put to death. He traveled by land through Asia Minor (modern day Turkey) under a Roman guard which he refers to as "ten leopards" in Rom 5:1. He stopped in Smyrna to visit his fellow bishop Polycarp and the church there under his care.[1] While at Smyrna Ignatius wrote to the churches in Ephesus, Magnesia, and Tralles, all in Asia Minor, as well as sending a missive to the church in Rome. The tenor of the *Letter to the Romans* suggests that there may have

---

1 Bart Ehrman assumes that Ignatius did not know Polycarp or the other bishops he mentions in his letters prior to his journey to Rome. See Ehrman *The Apostolic Fathers* (Cambridge, MA: Harvard University Press, 2003) p. 204. This is a gratuitous assumption. We simply do not know whether Ignatius was acquainted with the bishops of Asia Minor personally. In any case, his stress upon the divinely ordained authority of the bishop and his belief in the catholic nature of the church would have made him view them as his cohorts in faith. In this sense he would have known them even if he had never met them.

been some possibility of Ignatius's execution being stayed. He begs the Christians in Rome not to try to stop his martyrdom (see Rom 1:2; 2:1,2; 4:1-3). After visiting Smyrna, Ignatius traveled on to Troas where he wrote letters to the churches in Philadelphia and Smyrna along with a personal one to Polycarp. From Polycarp's *Letter to the Philippians* we learn that Ignatius stayed in Philippi for a while before moving on to Rome (13:2). This information is as much as we possess from the time of Ignatius himself.

The Martyrdom Itself

Eusebius tells us that Ignatius underwent martyrdom "in the tenth year of Trajan" (i.e. 107 or 108) but we don't know on what the date is based. Many nineteenth century scholars (e.g. Lightfoot, Harnack) thought that the martyrdom probably took place between 110-118. The accounts of the martyrdom from a later period come down to us in two forms: the *Antiochean Acts* and the *Roman Acts*. The *Roman Acts* are a more elaborate and hagiographic account. Most scholars see little historical value in this document. The *Antiochean Acts* are more restrained in their description and may contain some historical accuracy. Internal indications in both *Acts* suggest they came from the fourth century.

Though both *Acts* are intent upon glorifying Ignatius in a style typical of hagiographies, they do contain plausible passages which accord with other accounts of martyrdom in the second century such as the *Martyrdom of Polycarp*. Perhaps most striking is Ignatius's contempt for the present world which seems to have inspired many martyrs. When given the possibility of his being spared from torture, Ignatius responded that Christ was his only life. As he wrote in his letters, Christ for him was "true life" (Eph 11:1), his "constant life," (Eph 3:2), and his "pure light" (Rom 6:2).

Ignatius's Theology of Martyrdom

More important than the historical circumstances of Ignatius's death is his rich theology of martyrdom. From within the letters themselves we may glean many references to his impending death and its meaning for him. Earlier in chapter one we noticed how important being a disciple was for Ignatius. It seems that this was the most fundamental category through which he viewed his life. Careful contextual analysis reveals, however, that an integral part of discipleship for Ignatius was sharing in the passion of Jesus Christ. In Eph 1:2 he links reaching the arena in Rome with becoming a disciple. This awareness of being an incomplete disciple is contrasted with "becoming perfect in Jesus Christ" since he "possesses just the beginning of learning to be a disciple" (Eph 3:1). In the *Letter to the Magnesians* Ignatius wishes not only to be called a Christian but to be one in fact (4:1). The Christian has the "stamp of God the Father through Jesus Christ" (stamp = *character*) in Mag 5:2, a reference perhaps to the indelible mark of baptism.[2] One becomes a disciple through faithful participation in the mystery of Christ's death (Mag 9:1). However, it is in his *Letter to the Romans* that we find Ignatius's most poignant expressions of the connection between discipleship and martyrdom. In Rom 5:1 Ignatius sees

---

2 For an explanation of the Greek term *character* see the commentary at Mag 5:2.

his martyrdom as already beginning in his journey to Rome ("I fight the beasts from Syria to Rome") under the Roman guard ("ten leopards") conducting him to his destination. The injustices which he experiences at their hands are the means by which he is "becoming a disciple." These trials en route to Rome prepare his mind and heart; he is emboldened to ask the Romans to "coax the beasts into becoming his tomb" so that he can truly become "a disciple of Jesus Christ" (Rom 4:2). So, for Ignatius, martyrdom is not only a form of death; it is a way of life. It is the path to becoming a true disciple of Jesus Christ.

Ignatius's idea of martyrdom becomes clearer when we look at references to his chains.[3] His confined and constricted movements are in the name of Christ (Eph 3:1) and in Rom 1:1 Ignatius hopes to greet the Romans even though he is "bound in Christ Jesus." Rom 4:3 is especially significant:

> I do not command you as Peter and Paul did. They were apostles; I am a criminal. They were free but I am a slave even now. Rather, if I suffer I will be liberated for Jesus Christ and I will rise again free in him. For now I am learning as a prisoner to desire nothing else.

Here the contrast is not so much between Peter and Paul as apostles and Ignatius as a bishop but with Ignatius as a criminal (*katakritos*) which diminishes his power to command from a legal and social point of view. But such a worldly point of view contrasts with Ignatius's understanding that suffering makes him a person free for Jesus Christ. Such suffering in chains

---

3   Ignatius uses the verb *deo* ("bound") 14 (of 15) times to speak of himself as a prisoner. While some of the references to being bound are simply descriptive (e.g. Eph 21:2; Philad 5:1), several texts are embedded in a theology of martyrdom. The noun *desmos* ("chains") occurs 8 times in Ignatius's letters.

helps him desire nothing in this world.[4]

The contrast between being bound and being free surfaces again in Mag 12:1, "For since I am bound [in chains] I am not like even one of you who are at liberty. I know that you are not puffed up. You have Jesus Christ in you." Such language may appear as overly sentimental piety to a modern reader but in reality his criminal status has effected a greater depth of humility in Ignatius. This humility is preparing him for the final giving of his life. Ignatius sees his being under arrest as God's way of preparing him for the final test as the unusual phrase of Smyrn 11:1 has it, "bound in the most God-fitting chains."[5] This phrase seems to imply both that the chains in which the Romans have bound him are ultimately from God and that his bound status is most appropriate for his reaching God.

Being in chains, under guard, being thought a criminal, all these are only the martyrdom before the martyrdom for Ignatius. And Ignatius is conscious that his own life is lived on behalf of the church itself as he expresses it in Smyrn 10:2 and Polyc 2:3. Ignatius employs the word *antipsuchon* in close conjunction with *desmos* ("chains") in both texts: "My spirit and my bonds are your substitute soul" (Smyrn 10:2) and "I and my bonds that you love are your substitute soul in every way" (Polyc 2:3).[6] His sharing in the passion of Christ serves to advance

---

4   Cf. Rom 6:1, "it is better for me to die in Jesus Christ than to rule the ends of the earth."

5   Ehrman translates *dedemenos theoprepestatois desmois* as "chains that are most acceptable to God." See Ehrman at Smyrn 11:1.

6   BAG gives "ransom" as the meaning of *antipsuchon*. It does not occur in the NT nor in any other writings of the apostolic fathers. Ignatius's use seems to reflect his awareness of its etymological meaning "substitute soul." Ehrman rightly renders Smyrn 10:2, "My spirit is given in exchange for yours, as are my chains" and

the spiritual welfare of those to whom he writes since he is their "substitute soul" (*antipsuchon*). Since in his mind Ignatius's martyrdom began while still in chains, he is conscious that it is for more than his own salvation.

All this implies that martyrdom leads to eternal life in Ignatius's mind. He is aware of a reality beyond death, either for eternal blessing or eternal damnation.[7] Eternal life is connected with the death of Christ in Eph 7:2 ("the one physician ... brought ... true life in death") and in Mag 9:1 ("on this day, our life dawned through him and his death, which some deny"). Especially telling is Eph 18:1 in which Ignatius views the cross as the path to eternal life and his connection to it as a sacrifice of his life fitting for the sacrifice which Christ offered up: "My spirit is in sacrificial service for the cross, which is a scandal to unbelievers, but to us it is salvation and eternal life."

For Ignatius, then, martyrdom is more than the end of life, even more than the end of the Christian life. For him, martyrdom is a way of life because, as in the thought of Paul, Ignatius sees his life as flowing out of the life of Jesus Christ (cf. Gal 2:20). Ignatius views his union with the cross as his way not only to prepare for death but as carrying the death of Jesus Christ within himself (2 Cor 4:10).[8] And like John the apostle, Ignatius sees eternal life as the present possession of one who is united to Christ.[9] It is the presence of Christ's death within

---

Polyc 2:3, "I am given in exchange for you in every way."

7   Eph 16:2, "Such a man (i.e. one who corrupts through heresy) because he is defiled, will end up in unquenchable fire. The same is true for the one who listens to him."

8   In other texts Ignatius draws on the terminology of imitation to express the union of the church (and himself) with Christ. For a fuller explanation see chapter three.

9   For references to eternal life in the Johannine writings see Jn 1:4; 3:36; 5:24;

him that allows Ignatius to call himself "a substitute soul" (*antipsuchon*) and "a sacrificial offering" (*peripsema*) because he embraces the cross for the benefit of the members of the body of Christ. His whole life — his chains and his mistreatment — constitutes a sacrificial martyrdom for Christ and for the church.[10]

6:40; 11:25; 14:6.

10 Camelot summarizes Ignatius's view of martyrdom well, "For the martyr death is not only giving witness to the truth, nor is it the supreme gesture of love. It is the reproduction of the death of Christ." Camelot, p. 33.

Chapter Three
Christ and Redemption in the Theology of Ignatius

The centrality of Christ in the theology of Ignatius implied in chapter two becomes all the clearer when the designations of Christ are examined more carefully. Jesus Christ is called "the beloved of the Father" (Smyrn Sal); he is the "shared hope" of Christians (Philad 11:2), and for those same believers he is "our true life" (Smyrn 4:1) and "the perfect hope" (Smyrn 10:2).[1] In light of the docetic tendencies threatening the churches of Asia Minor, Ignatius repeatedly emphasizes the union of the timeless and eternal Christ with the historical and physical reality of Jesus (see Eph 7; Polyc 3:2). In short, Jesus Christ is the center of the gospel and the criterion to distinguish truth from falsehood (Philad 6:1; 8:2). Yet none of Ignatius's specific designations for Jesus Christ gets to the heart of Ignatius's christology like his emphasis on the union of the Word with the Father.

---

1   Some MSS of Smyrn 10:2 have "perfect faith."

Jesus Christ as True God and True Man

Nothing speaks of Ignatius's view of the relation of Jesus to the Father more eloquently than when he says in Mag 1:2 "the most important union is ... that of Jesus and the Father." This union with the Father is the basis of Ignatius's explicit language about Jesus Christ as God. In several texts Ignatius glosses Jesus Christ with the addition "God" or "our God" (Eph Sal; 18:2; Trall 7:1; Rom Sal; 3:3; Polyc 8:3). In the first chapter of the *Letter to the Smyrneans* Ignatius explicitly says, "I glorify Jesus Christ, the God who made you" (Smyrn 1:1).

Even more important for Ignatius is the true humanity of Christ in light of the Docetism which he and other church leaders faced. Docetism denied the true humanity of Christ and so Ignatius defines the gospel as a proclamation of the flesh of Jesus Christ (Philad 5:1, "while I flee for refuge in the gospel as to the flesh of Jesus") since in that flesh he suffered (Smyrn 1:2, "Truly he was nailed [to the cross] in the flesh for us") and rose again from the dead (Smyrn 3:1, "I know and believe that he was in the flesh after the resurrection"). Especially striking is the credal-like first chapter of the *Letter to the Smyrneans* wherein Ignatius recounts the plan of salvation manifested in Jesus Christ. The gospel consists not only in the historical events of Christ's life that Ignatius recounts but also in the union of the faithful with those events:

> I know that you have been prepared in an unshakeable faith, as you were nailed to the cross of the Lord Jesus Christ in flesh and spirit and established in love in the blood of Christ, having been fulfilled for our Lord (Smyrn 1:1).

Then, as if to reassure the faithful at Smyrna that their partici-

pation in the Paschal Mystery is not an illusion, he reminds
them that Jesus Christ was "truly born of a virgin," that he was
"baptized by John to fulfill all righteousness," that "he was truly
nailed [to the cross] in the flesh for us under Pontius Pilate and
Herod the tetrarch," that "he might carry a standard for the
ages through the resurrection for his holy and faithful ones"
and finally that he was to reconcile Jew and Gentile "in the one
body of his church" (Smyrn 1). This emphasis on the historical
reality of Christ's life grounds not only the participation of the
faithful but also the inseparable connection between Christ and
the church.[2]

Throughout the seven letters Ignatius returns repeatedly to
the historical truth of the Incarnation of the Son of God. The
Incarnation plays a variety of roles in different contexts. As in
the case of the Smyrneans, Ignatius stresses that the Magnesians
ought to be fully convinced of the historical truthfulness of
Jesus's life (Mag 11:1). But in Mag 13:2 the earthly life of Jesus
Christ becomes a model of submission: "be subject to your
bishop and to one another, as Jesus Christ in the flesh is to the
Father." The same emphasis with a liturgical dimension appears
in Eph 20:2 where Ignatius specifically ties the earthly life of
Jesus to the healing purpose of the Eucharist as the "medicine
of immortality." In the previous chapter Ignatius places the virgin birth in a cosmic context in which Jesus's earthly existence
is a manifestation of the "silence of God" (Eph 19: 1, 2). Finally,
the main purpose of Jesus's Incarnation shows up in Eph 7:2
where as the "one physician" he is said to be:

---

2   Trall 9:1 also emphasizes the historical veracity of Jesus's life.

fleshly and spiritual
born and unborn
God coming in the flesh
in death, true life
from Mary and from God
first suffering and then beyond suffering.

These contrasting pairs summarize the apparent paradoxes of the Incarnation. Nor are these antinomies played down by Ignatius or any of the later fathers of the church because in them resides the mystery of the most unique reality in all human history — the true and living God taking upon himself a fully human nature. All the elements in Ignatius's doctrines of the church and the Eucharist flow out of the Incarnation.

The Paschal Mystery: Christ's Redemptive Work

If Christ stands at the center of Ignatius's whole theology, the Paschal Mystery stands at the center of his whole theology of Christ. Without his death and resurrection, the entire life of Jesus Christ holds no significance for the world or for the church. Look again at Smyrn 1:2 where Ignatius says that Jesus Christ suffered his "God-blessed passion (*pathos*) in order to carry a standard for his holy and faithful ones through the resurrection." Drawing on the imagery of Isaiah 5:26, Ignatius intends to stress that the cross and all its suffering constitutes the signal (or battle standard) of God's kingdom brought to fulfillment in the resurrection. Smyrn 2:1 shows how important the historical reality of Christ's suffering is: "*And all these things* he suffered for our sake to save us. And truly he suffered just as he also truly raised himself." For Ignatius, any denial or mitigation of the passion is in effect to relinquish the message of the gospel.

The historical reality of Christ's death is manifested significantly by Ignatius's imagery in Eph 9:1,2:

> As stones of the Father's temple you have been prepared to be God the Father's building, lifted up to the heights through the crane of Jesus Christ, which is the cross, as you use the Holy Spirit for a rope. Your faith is your guide; love is the way that carries you up to God.

No writer in the New Testament speaks of the passion as a crane (*machane*) but the signification is clear. The cross serves as the only instrument which can bridge the gap between heaven and earth. Contrary to its appearance, the shameful death of the cross carries one upward into the heights (*anapheromenoi eis ta hupse*). Here we have the objective and subjective aspects of redemption linked in an intimate way. The cross is the objective work of redemption; the Holy Spirit is the interior but still objective "rope" (*schoinion*) drawing the faithful up on the cross while the subjective virtues of faith and love carry them up to God. Without the cross and the Spirit, faith and love are illusory because they have no contact with real history. On the other hand, the passion and the Spirit do not fulfill their proper purpose without faith and love in the church. In this way Ignatius sees the Paschal events as true mysteries, i.e. as historical realities embodying the invisible powers of faith and love available to the church.

The Application of Christ's Redemption

To consider the work of Christ in the accomplishment of redemption through the Paschal Mystery implies another question: what does this work of Christ do for the actual salvation of the human race? For Ignatius, these two questions are intimately bound up with each other. We noted in chapter one that Ignatius views himself and all believers through the primary lens of discipleship. This category is both a present fact and the future goal of the Christian, or in Pauline terms, the "already" and the "not yet" of salvation. This fundamental reality causes him to pose the question, "How can we live without him whom the prophets, since they were his disciples by the Spirit, were expecting as their teacher?" (Mag 9:2). In this rhetorical question, Ignatius ponders the meaning of true life who is Jesus Christ (Mag 9:1). That life from Christ produces hope, or, as Christ is simply called in Mag 11:1 and Trall 2:2, "our hope."

The application of redemption to the individual in salvation finds its roots in the union of Christ with the church. That is why Ignatius confidently asserts that Jesus Christ is the "new leaven" (Mag 10:2). He has instituted the new Passover (Eucharist) which requires the removal of the old leaven of Judaism.[3] This also explains why for Ignatius obedience to rightful authority in the church (bishop, presbyters, and deacons) is so important. It is by union with the church that one has a valid Eucharist and therefore the saving power of Christ's body (Philad 4:1; Smyrn 8:1, 2).

For Ignatius, as the individual is connected to the church and draws grace from the sacraments (baptism and Eucharist), salvation becomes more a reality in his life. In Eph 1:1 Ignatius alludes to baptism when he speaks of obtaining "the highly loved name [of God] by a just nature in accord with the faith and love in Christ Jesus." That just nature allows the faithful "to be filled with

---

3   Ignatius's allusion to the new Passover probably draws on Paul's similar expressions in 1 Cor 5:7, 8.

God" (Mag 14:1) by participating in the historical mysteries of Christ's life (Mag 11:1). Baptism obtains the just nature by receiving "the stamp (*character*) of God the Father in love through Jesus Christ." The indelible mark of baptism distinguishes the faithful from the world (Mag 5:1, 2). As with Paul who teaches in Rom 6:1ff that baptism unites the baptized to the passion and resurrection of Christ, so Ignatius reminds the Magnesians that "if we do not willingly embrace dying for his passion, his life is not in us" (Mag 5:2). Ignatius expresses this union with Christ in the Paschal Mystery as his highest goal in Trall 4:2 when he says, "I love suffering but I don't know if I am worthy."

The centrality of Christ's passion again plays a dominant role in Ignatius's theology of salvation through his language of reaching or attaining to God.[4] If baptism is the beginning of salvation in Ignatius's thought, attaining to God through martyrdom is the culmination of his journey. Thus he asks the Magnesians to remember him in their prayers that he may attain to God and to the level of holiness resident in the Syrian church (Mag 14:1). He so fervently desires to do battle with the beasts in Rome because he knows that this is his means of attaining to God (Rom 4:1). Attaining to the grace to share Christ's death (see Rom 1:2) leads to attaining Jesus Christ himself (Rom 5:3). Yet Ignatius's ability to reach God is also linked to the prayers he asks of his recipients (Philad 5:1; Smyrn 11:1). And Ignatius returns the grace in answer to their prayers by purifying himself in sacrifice for his hearers, "my spirit makes you pure not only now but also when I attain to God" (Trall 13:3).[5]

---

4   The word *epitugchano* ("reaching" or "attaining" to God) occurs 19 times in the Ignatian corpus and always in the aorist tense (*epitucho*) which carries a punctiliar sense of finality.

5   This verse can be translated several different ways. See comments at Trall 13:3.

Since becoming a disciple and obtaining salvation are a work in progress for Ignatius, this work implies the obligation to grow in the virtues which Christ himself displayed in his earthly life. Following the Pauline model, Ignatius finds both negative and positive dimensions to the process.[6] The Christian must reject the evil influences of the world and imitate the positive virtues of Christ. Ignatius praises the Roman church for its purity when he speaks of it as "filled with God's grace without distinction, and strained off from every foreign color" (Rom Sal). And Ignatius offers his own attitude as a model when he later says to the Romans, "For now I am learning as a prisoner to desire nothing" other than Christ (Rom 4:3). On the positive side, Ignatius points the Trallians to the example of their bishop Polybius whose love and "very bearing is a great instruction" and whose "meekness is [his] power" (Trall 3:2).

Christ and his redemption, then, form the ultimate ground of Ignatius's theology. The martyrdom of the bishop of Antioch, the Eucharist, the hierarchical structure of the church, salvation, and the development of Christian virtue all have no meaning without Christ and his Paschal Mystery. Christ is the center around which everything in Ignatius's theology revolves. The church and its unity for which he is so zealous has no existence or purpose without the truth Paul proclaimed, i.e. that Christ is the head and the church his body.

---

6 Paul in Eph 4:22-24 employs the language of "putting off the old self" and "putting on the new self."

Chapter Four
The Church in the Ignatian Letters

The church in the Ignatian epistles is a multi-faceted entity which must be viewed from several different vantage points to be fully understood. It is clear that Ignatius's greatest concern is the unity of Christ's body as an essential mark (*character*) of the church. Out of this unity with Christ and with one another, the members of the church grow toward God. The very nature of the church yields its structure. The church is both an organism and an organization. These two aspects influence and reinforce one another in Ignatius's thought.

In the language of Ignatius, how do we know what refers to the nature (essence) of the church and what refers to its structure? His copious use of the terms bishop (*episkopos*), presbyter (*presbuteros*), and deacon (*diakonos*) obviously has to do with the structure of the church. His many exhortations to obedience and submission to the bishop and presbytery (e.g. Eph 2:2; 5:3; Trall 2:1,2; 13:2; Polyc 6:1) reinforce his ideal of a church unified in belief and practice around the central figure of the bishop. The appearance of this strong language of hierarchical episcopacy at such an early date in the history of Christianity has surprised readers for centuries. Many scholars (e.g. Walter Bauer) have seen this emphasis on the monepiscopacy in Ignatius as a departure from the collaborative structure of the church which they see in the NT. As Ehrman put it, "in the early modern period it was precisely this witness to the monepiscopacy at such an early date that drove scholars to determine whether Ignatius of Antioch had in fact penned all, or some, or any of the letters that appear under his name."[1] Those who questioned Ignatian authorship were motivated by their prior conception of the church as a more democratic organization in its earliest stages of development. Naturally, those who believed that the NT authorized the episcopacy had no reason to doubt the authenticity of the claims of Ignatian authorship found in the letters.

The question then facing the reader of these letters has to do with how this monepiscopal structure of the church in Ignatius relates to other aspects of his ecclesiology. It is precisely here that the interpreter's presuppositions can influence how he assembles and interprets the evidence. I would suggest that the key to understanding Ignatius's view of the church lies in his broader concept of unity: the unity of God, the unity of Christ, unity with God, with Christ, with the bishop, presbyters, and deacons. This unity is first and foremost a mystical one. It is not a unity within one locale or bishopric; it is an organic unity which flows from God himself and which is communicated through the sacrament of the Eucharist. The structure of the

---

1   Bart D. Ehrman (editor and translator) *The Apostolic Fathers* (Cambridge, MA: Harvard University Press, 2003) vol. 1, p. 203.

church flows out of that unity. The four marks of the church later codified in the Nicene Creed (one, holy, catholic, and apostolic) are all present in Ignatius's letters and provide us with a convenient organizing principle to understand his theology of the church.

The Unity of the Church

Ignatius thinks of the church as a divine organism and organization. Unity is essential to the welfare of the church, a unity which is expressed in obedience to the lawful bishop of a particular church. Being in submission to the bishop implies being in union with the presbyters and deacons under his leadership. At the same time unity is not a matter of outward and formalistic subjection; it is rather a living reality that is connected to the proper celebration of the sacraments, especially the Eucharist. A eucharistic celebration is valid precisely because it is under a legitimate bishop of the church (Smyrn 8). The Eucharist does not, however, derive its efficacy from the bishop. It is because the Eucharist is the flesh of Jesus Christ (Smyrn 7:1) that faith, hope, and love are obtainable virtues for the faithful. The bishop is the guarantor of a valid sacrament but the sacrament itself provides the true supernatural unity for the church.

The Letter to the Philadelphians provides us with an appropriate window on the Ignatian view of unity. Ignatius's main word for unity (*henosis*) occurs eight times in the entire corpus, three of which occur in this letter. Philad 7:2 has the Christian obligation simply to "love unity" and "to flee divisions." Being "an imitator of Christ, as he was of his Father" is the ultimate ground for seeking unity and eschewing divisions within the church. In the following chapter (8:1) Ignatius characterizes himself as a man "set on unity" (*eis henosin katertismenos*). This unity is so serious that repentance entails coming back to the same unity abandoned by those who have left the church. Ignatius's phrase, "to the unity of God" (*eis henoteta theou*) in Philad 8:1 likely means the unity which God gives to the church. It is linked immediately with "the council of the bishop" because the bishop is the representative of the Father (cf. Mag 6:1 "the bishop presides in the place of God").

Such exhortations to unity are not divorced from what he says earlier in *Philadelphians* when he commands, "Be diligent to use only one Eucharist. For there is only one flesh of our Lord Jesus Christ and one cup for unity in his blood" (4:1). The fourth chapter asserts in no uncertain terms that sacramental and governmental unity imply one another. Acting in accord with God's will (*kata theon*) means being in attendance at the "one altar" established by the bishop. The Eucharist is the tangible source of unity for the church in this world for one cannot be certain that there is a valid Eucharist apart from the legitimate authority of the bishop. The ultimate source of the church's unity is God himself, or as Ignatius puts it in Trall 11:2, "the head cannot be born without the members because God promises that unity which is himself."

Ignatius's longest letter addressed to the church of Ephesus also has much on unity though here the Bishop of Antioch uses a synonym of the word he used in *Philadelphians* (*henotes*). The entire fourth chapter focuses on the unity and harmony of fraternal charity in the church:

> (1) Therefore, it is fitting that you agree with the opinion of
> the bishop as you are doing. Your rightly famous presbytery

is worthy of God. It is in harmony with the bishop like strings tuned to a harp. For this reason, Jesus Christ is praised in your harmony and in your united love. (2) Now, all of you, become a chorus together that by a united voice in harmony as you take up the tune of God in unity, you may sing in one voice through Jesus Christ to the Father. This is so that the Father may hear and recognize you by the good things you do, you who are members of his Son. So, it is useful for you to be in blameless unity that you may always partake of God (Eph 4).

The musical language used here may allude to the liturgy of the church as Ignatius knew it, since he speaks about Jesus Christ being praised in harmony (*homonoia* = united mind) and symphonic love (*sunphono agape*). Clearly, as in his other epistles, Ignatius in *Ephesians* sees harmony, love, and union with the bishop as intimately intertwined with a proper liturgical and sacramental life. All this emphasis on unity has the goal (*telos*) of "partaking always in God" (*theou pantote metechete*).

Ephesians employs other terms to express this unity with God and the bishop. In chapter five we hear Ignatius offering his blessing (*makarizo*)[2] to the Ephesians because the faithful there are mingled with (*egkerannumi*) the bishop as Christ is with the Father (5:1). The comparison between earth and heaven is reminiscent of the Johannine prayer of Jesus "that they may be one just as we are one" (Jn 17:21). The unity of the faithful with their shepherds is based on a divine relation of Jesus Christ to the Father in the Trinity. We gain a further insight into the origin of unity in God from 14:1, "you have faith and love which is the beginning and end of life. The beginning is faith; the end is love. Once the two are in unity

---

2 See the discussion below on *makarizo* and my commentary on Eph 5:1.

it is God." Ignatius's exhortation to embrace both faith and love arises from his belief that faith and love are already one in God himself. Living in faith and love is possible if God dwells in the believer (see Eph 15:3) and if the faithful act in love toward one another (21:1).

The Holiness of the Church

The unity of the church also implies its holiness. Holiness comes to expression in Ignatius's letters as it might in any occasional writing that is primarily addressing other topics. In the salutations of each letter Ignatius uses terms designating holiness in one way or another. When Ignatius speaks of the Ephesian church as "unified and chosen in true suffering" and greets it "in blameless joy" he is drawing on the Pauline terms "chosen" and "blameless" as ways of speaking of holiness (Eph Sal).[3] The Magnesian church he designates as "blessed in the grace of God in Christ Jesus our Savior" (Mag Sal). And members of the church at Philadelphia are described by Ignatius as those whom God "established according to his own will in confirmation by the Holy Spirit" (Philad Sal). Sometimes the word "holy" occurs as the church is called "holy ... chosen ... worthy of God" (Trall Sal). Even more explicitly we hear Ignatius greeting the church in Smyrna as one "most worthy of God and bearing holiness (*hagiophoro*)" (Smyrn Sal).

The mark of holiness is drawn out further by Ignatius in his notion of sharing graces in the body of Christ. This was implied in his self-designation as servant and slave of Christ. It was con-

---

3   Later, too, in Eph 9:2 Ignatius says, "you are fellow travelers, bearing God and bearing a temple, Christ-bearers, bearers of holiness (*hagiophoroi*), etc."

tained in his profession of being a disciple while seeking even more to follow Christ to martyrdom. However, there are even clearer indications of the sharing of holiness present in his use of the unusual words *antipsuchon* (four times) and *peripsema* (twice). Earlier I translated *antipsuchon* as "substitute soul" but now we must carefully examine it in the context of its occurrences. Ignatius uses it twice in his *Letter to Polycarp*. In 2:3 he says, "I and my bonds that you love are your substitute soul in every way. " In this context Ignatius exhorts Polycarp to be a wise and faithful shepherd who will weather the storms of opposition. To show his solidarity with Polycarp, Ignatius reminds the Smyrnean bishop that he is united with him in every respect (*kata panta*), so much so in fact, that Ignatius and his chains are a means of his sharing in Polycarp's ministry while Polycarp also shares in the martyrdom that Ignatius will face. Their being an *antipsuchon* for each other represents the highest form of Christian love. Of course, the emphasis of the text lies on Ignatius being an *antipsuchon* for Polycarp but in Polyc 6:1 Ignatius changes the alignment slightly so that he is the *antipsuchon* for those who are subject to bishop Polycarp.[4] And in his letter to the same congregation he offers a similar expression, "my spirit and my bonds are your substitute soul" (Smyrn 10:2). There is no doubt that for Ignatius holiness implies obedience to the rightful bishop. Ignatius is offering his imprisonment and chains as a substitute for the members of the church. His submissive spirit in obedience to God through his imprisonment will

---

4   In chapter 6, Ignatius changes the form of his exhortations from singular to plural, a fact that may puzzle some in a personal letter to one bishop. However, even letters addressed to individuals in ancient Christianity also served as instruction for a wider audience.

engender holiness in the members of the Smyrnean church as they too learn submission. The last occurrence is found in Eph 21:1, "I am your substitute soul and also for those whom you sent to Smyrna for the honor of God." Occurring in a small chapter of farewell wishes, such a heavy theological term seems out of place. However, in the sentences just preceding, Ignatius speaks of the "breaking of one bread" as "the medicine of immortality, the antidote against death" (Eph 20:2). As these words evoke the liturgy in the minds of his readers, Ignatius could naturally think of himself as a substitute soul for his recipients because Christ in the liturgy acts as a substitute victim for others.[5] The underlying theme in all these instances of "substitute soul" (*antipsuchon*) is that of the giving and receiving of holiness among the members of the church.

The notion of substitution is even more evident in the two instances of *peripsema*, both of which occur in the *Letter to the Ephesians*. In 18:1 Ignatius says, "my spirit is a *peripsema* of the cross." My translation at 18:1 uses "sacrificial service" whereas I use the colloquialism "scum of the earth" at 8:1. The word *peripsema* is difficult to translate but it seems to carry the connotations of something vile. In Eph 18:1 the meaning is explained further by the cross in that Ignatius's spirit experiences the vileness of the cross which is a scandal to unbelievers. In Eph 8:1 this vileness of the cross is conjoined with Ignatius's desire to share holiness with the Ephesians by his own sanctification, "As scum of the earth I sanctify myself for you Ephesians, for the church famous for ages." Together, *antipsuchon* ("substitute soul") and *peripsema* ("sacrificial substitute") suggest a man who has devoted himself to the spiritual welfare of others and

---

5   For Camelot's explanation of *antipsuchon* at Eph 21:1 see Camelot p. 79.

who shares his holiness for the benefit of the church.

The Catholicity of the Church

Ignatius is the first Christian writer we know of to use the term "catholic church" (Smyrn 8:2). In the context of the *Letter to the Smyrneans,* Ignatius urges his readers to live in obedience to their bishop Polycarp. Attempting to underscore the divine authority of the episcopal office, Ignatius says:

> (1) You all should follow the bishop as Jesus Christ does the Father. Follow too the presbytery as the apostles, and honor the deacons as the command of God. Let no one do anything that is proper for the church without the bishop. Let that Eucharist be considered valid that is under the bishop or performed by one to whom he entrusts it. (2) Wherever the bishop appears, let the fullness [of the church] be as *wherever Christ Jesus appears, there is the catholic church.* It is not lawful to baptize or to hold an agape feast without the bishop. On the other hand, what he approves is pleasing to God so that everything that is practiced may be certain and valid (Smyrn 8:1,2).

The phrase *katholike ecclesia,* of course, means "universal church" but explicating its deeper theological meaning reveals how different theologies of the church approach the task of explaining this phrase. There can be no doubt that this instance of the word *katholikos* being applied to the church leads to its later usage in the Nicene creed ("I believe in one, holy, catholic, and apostolic church"). From Ignatius in the early second century to Nicea in the early fourth, the usage of the word grows through time. The word occurs later in the second century in the *Martyrdom of Polycarp* (about forty years later). In the salutation of that document the phrase is expanded by the writer "to all those sojourners of the holy and catholic church in every place." Similarly, the author speaks of "the whole catholic church throughout the known world" (Mart Polyc 8:1) and of Polycarp as the bishop of the "catholic church in Smyrna" (Mart Polyc 16:2). Historically, most Protestant scholars read this phrase with a non-organizational meaning. In their minds, it is simply the universal church and carries no connotation of the Catholic Church centered in the See of Rome. Catholic scholars have historically seen the phrase as simply the beginnings of the sense of catholicity which comes to fuller expression in, say, Cyprian of Carthage in the mid-third century.[6]

To navigate between these interpretative tendencies one must avoid two extremes. One is anachronism, that is, the attribution of later meanings back into earlier texts; the other is failing to trace the development of the term *katholikos* from Ignatius to its later usage in the third and fourth centuries. Protestant scholars tend to accuse Catholic historians of the former mistake while Catholic scholars tend to accuse Protestants of the latter. And this is no idle debate. The truly Christian concept of the church is at stake and the differences account for why Protestants and Catholics have such varying doctrines of the church. Clearly, we must pay close attention to the text of Ignatius's *Letter to the Smyrneans* where the phrase *katholike ecclesia* occurs for the first time. The two correlative clauses of Smyrn 8:2 give some indication of its intended meaning, "Wherever the bishop appears, let

---

6   Cyprian wrote *On the Unity of the Catholic Church* (*De unitate ecclesiae catholicae*) in the mid-third century. This is evidence that the term "catholic" had become a standard appellation by that time. While Latin Christians were aware of the word being an adjective borrowed from Greek, its use as a title of the church shows it had acquired a kind of proper-name status as opposed to simply meaning "universal."

there be the fullness [of the church] as *wherever Christ Jesus appears, there is the catholic church.*" The parallel between the bishop and Christ Jesus, so frequent and familiar in other Ignatian texts, shows that for Ignatius the church and its fullness has little to do with numbers or geography.[7] The comparison turns on locality versus universality: the bishop is the fullness of the local church (diocese) while Christ Jesus is the fullness of the whole church. The command to obey the bishop in liturgical matters immediately following ("It is not lawful to baptize or to hold an agape feast without the bishop") shows that this is also more than a simple analogy. For Ignatius, the bishop embodies Christ Jesus on a local level. The bishop is the human and physical representative of Christ to a particular church. The choice of "catholic" to describe the church is inspired by the universality of Christ's salvation in the NT. Christ intended the church to be for people of every nation, language, and ethnic group (cf. Mt 28:19; Mk 16:15; Rev 5:9,10). The church being catholic, therefore, is not only an occasional description but is an essential feature of the church Christ founded.

The development of the sense of catholicity continues in the *Martyrdom of Polycarp*. When the author speaks of "the whole catholic church throughout the known world" in Mart Polyc 8:1, the addition of "whole" or "all" (*pases*) suggests that for him there is a need to specify the universality of the church that is

---

7   Ehrman translates the relevant phrase, "Let the congregation be wherever the bishop is; just as wherever Jesus Christ is, there also is the universal church." *The Apostolic Fathers* vol. 1 p. 305. It has been traditional to translate "fullness" (*plethos*) as "congregation" or "community" and there is no doubt justification for this translation. In Smyrn 8:2, however, the original sense of *plethos* ("fullness") can be retained, meaning both the fullness of the local church and fullness in a deeper sense of the mystical body.

not completely expressed in the term "catholic." The adjective "catholic" has now become more like a proper noun describing something inherent to the nature of the church. Here the term anticipates later developments that lead to the confession of the church as holy and catholic, a truth already evident in the Salutation of the *Martyrdom of Polycarp*, "to all those sojourners of the holy and catholic church in every place." (Mart Polyc Sal). So "catholic" describes not just the quality of universality but is a proper designation of the church. Thus the *Martyrdom of Polycarp* also speaks of Polycarp as a bishop of the "catholic church in Smyrna," perhaps to distinguish it from other competing bodies within Smyrna which claim to have the true apostolic teaching.

Is it possible that this distinction is present in Ignatius's *Letter to the Smyrneans* in 8:2 when he says, "wherever Christ Jesus is, there is the catholic church?" Was Ignatius using the term "catholic" to distinguish the church under Polycarp from heretical groups in Smyrna claiming apostolic authority? It is in fact highly likely that he had this meaning in mind. Chapter 7 of the *Letter to the Smyrneans* is about such a group. Ignatius says that they will not submit to Polycarp's leadership by joining with the church in its eucharistic celebration and prayers (Smyrn 7:1). The faithful must abstain from this group as the dissidents abstain from the church. To be unified one must avoid divisions (Smyrn 7:2). Then, in Smyrn 8:1, Ignatius reinforces structural unity by emphasizing obedience and liturgical validity. So, in Smyrn 8:2, when Ignatius uses the phrase "catholic church," he probably has a meaning in mind which distinguishes the church from the dissident group(s) in Smyrna. Thus, already in the beginning of the second century the phrase *katholike ecclesia* probably means more than simply "the whole church" or "the universal church." It denotes the church which has valid bishops appointed by or in the true line of succession from the apostles. This church was intended by Christ to be "catholic" (i.e. for the whole world) because Christ himself was intended for the whole of humanity.

The Apostolicity of the Church

Among modern scholars of early Christianity we find the most disparate perspectives in their consideration of apostolicity in early witnesses such as Ignatius, Clement of Rome, and the author of the *Didache.* I suggested earlier that unity is the hallmark of Ignatius's view of the church because he grounds the other marks of the church in its being a unified body established by Christ. The church must be holy, catholic, and apostolic because it is the one body on earth which arose out of a divine commission given by Christ and because it alone carries on the salvific mission of Christ into the whole world.

Thus far I have argued that Ignatius's view of unity is rooted in the other unities he affirms or assumes. The unity of the triune God is to be reflected in the church; the unity of Christ in his human and divine natures forms the structure of the church in its outward ("fleshly") and inward ("spiritual") dimensions. The orders of ministry such as episcopate, presbyterate, and diaconate are the structured forms through which Christ shepherds the church.

The answer to the question of why Ignatius sees the structure of the church as he does and of what importance that episcopal structure holds for modern views of the church remains of vital practical importance. The unities mentioned above, of course, provide the beginnings of an answer but not all early church scholars see Ignatius in the same light. One of the most telling differences exists between those who see Ignatius's witness to the episcopacy as an inherent feature of the early church and those who see his views as one among many that may or may not have been shared by others. For example, the well-respected patristic scholar Boniface Ramsey once wrote, "Just because Ignatius of Antioch, to take one famous example, emphasizes the role of bishop in the early second-century churches of Antioch and Asia Minor does not mean that anyone else felt the same way about the bishop at that time, or even that bishops existed in other churches at such an early period."[8] Ramsey here expresses a view common among modern scholars of the early church, a view that has roots in the nineteenth-century liberalism epitomized in the theology of Adolf Harnack.

In this view, Ignatius does not stand as a witness to the faith of the early second century church but as one holding to a somewhat idiosyncractic view of the structure of the church. One who articulated this atomistic approach in a fashion that still remains influential today is Walter Bauer. In chapter three of his 1934 book *Orthodoxy and Heresy in Earliest Christianity* Bauer discusses Ignatius and Polycarp.[9] Bauer assumes without argument that there was no need for a monarchical episcopacy prior to the problems of heresy facing Ignatius. He saw the rise of a

---

8   Boniface Ramsey *Beginning to Read the Fathers* (New York: Paulist Press, 1985) p. 10. Ramsey does proceed to outline some common themes among the fathers but these theme are more problems they all addressed than beliefs they shared in common.

9   A second edition of Bauer's book was issued in German in 1964 and was only recently translated into English. The translated portions I quote are from that of Gerhard Krodel online.

hierarchical structure advocated by Ignatius as necessary only when a more collaborative form of church government failed to deal with problems. Bauer tends to see the issue only in terms of the exercise of power.

The most prominent feature of the Ignatian letters which makes Bauer's view of early Christianity problematic is the manner in which Ignatius discusses the episcopate, the presbytery, and the diaconate. First, his exhortations to obedience display a sense of divine obligation arising out of the divine appointment of the clergy. It is not simply that the bishop is the most effective means to handle the problem of heterodoxy or that Ignatius desires to assert the power of the bishop in the face of revolt. The justifications offered by Ignatius do not lie in anything pragmatic or autocratic. The main word for obedience (*hupotassomai*) occurs eight times in the Ignatian letters along with other expressions which imply that obedience to the clergy is an obligation given by God himself. In Eph 2:2, Ignatius connects obedience to unity and the pursuit of holiness: "that, knit together in a single obedience, you may be holy in every respect by being subject to the bishop and to the presbytery." And later in the same letter Ignatius says, "So let us be diligent not to oppose the bishop that we may be subject to God" (Eph 5:3). In exhorting Polycarp's congregation at Smyrna Ignatius makes this explicit again: "Pay attention to the bishop that God may do the same to you" (Polyc 6:1). For Ignatius, the blessing of God is tied intimately to the bishop and the presbytery. The ease with which Ignatius can speak of obedience to rightful authority and love among members of the church shows how deeply he thinks that obedience arises from divine obligation: "Farewell in Jesus Christ. Be subject to the bishop as you are to the commandment; and likewise to the presbytery. Love each and every one with an undivided heart" (Trall 13:2). Yet the most explicit expression of this theme is to be found earlier in the *Letter to the Trallians*:

> When you are submissive to the bishop as to Jesus Christ, you seem to me to be living not in accord with human [custom] but in accord with Jesus Christ who died for us. This was so that by believing in his death you may escape dying. As is already your practice, it is necessary to do nothing without [the approval of] the bishop, but to be submissive to the presbytery as to the apostles of Jesus Christ, our hope (Trall 2:1,2).

Grounding these commands in obedience to God shows very clearly that for Ignatius the structure of the church is not of human origin. To disobey the bishop or the presbyters is to disobey God. If one seeks to be a disciple of Jesus Christ, one must live in submission to the proper authorities established within the church.

Second, there are other indications in Ignatius's letters that this divine authority in the church came through the apostles, and that such apostolic authority continues through the ministry of bishops. In the Salutation of the *Letter to the Trallians* we find an interesting phrase: "I greet you in the fullness, in apostolic authority, and I wish you the warmest greetings" (Trall Sal). The phrase in question in Greek is *en apostoliko characteri*. Most translations render this phrase "in an apostolic manner" or some equivalent, as if Ignatius is only following the pattern set by the apostles in the letters of the NT.[10] The question here revolves around whether the term *character* means "manner."

---

10 Thus, Bauer/Paulsen, Camelot, Ehrman, Holmes, and Lightfoot.

Walter Bauer classified the meaning of this text under "characteristic trait or manner ... distinctive mark" in his famous lexicon of NT Greek and the early fathers although he renders *character* in Heb 1:3 as "exact representation."[11] The famous early church scholar of the late nineteenth century, J.B. Lightfoot, explained the phrase as following the "precedent set in the apostolic epistles."[12] My translation "in apostolic authority" claims more than simply following a pattern of greeting started by the apostles. It sees Ignatius greeting the Trallians with an apostolic authority.

The word *character* probably means more than "manner" or "fashion." It certainly means more in the other two instances where Ignatius uses the term, both of which are in the *Letter to the Magnesians* 5:2. Here it undeniably means "stamp" or "impression" since it occurs in a context of coinage:

> As there are two types of coins, one of God and the other of the world and each of them has a stamp on them, [so] unbelievers have that of the world, and believers have the stamp of God the Father in love through Jesus Christ (Mag 5:2).

Here it bears the strong meaning evident in Heb 1:3 when the biblical author speaks of the Son as "the outshining of glory and the exact representation (stamp) of his being." In none of these other contexts is the term *character* demoted in meaning to "manner." The main reason that *character* is translated and interpreted as "manner" in the salutation of the *Letter to the Trallians* is that Ignatius elsewhere appears to deny his own apostolic authority. Bauer explicitly says that Ignatius is not

---

11 BAG p. 884.
12 J.B. Lightfoot *The Apostolic Fathers: Clement, Ignatius, Polycarp* vol. 2, pp. 152,153.

claiming apostolic authority, which he sees as excluded by Ignatius's own words in Trall 3:3 and Rom 4:3.[13] Lightfoot too, appealing to Theodor Zahn earlier, says that if Ignatius meant apostolic authority here in the salutation, he would be contradicting himself, because in Trall 3:3 Ignatius says, "I did not think that since I am condemned I could command you like an apostle." And the common interpretation seems to garner support from Paul's *Letter to the Romans*:

> I do not command you as Peter and Paul did. They were apostles; I am a criminal. They were free but I am a slave even now. Rather, if I suffer I will be liberated for Jesus Christ and I will rise again free in him. For now I am learning as a prisoner to desire nothing [else] (Rom 4:3).

Yet, it seems to me that these scholars have hastily followed a tradition that misses the main contrast present in these three texts (Trall Sal; 3:3; Rom 4:3). As I pointed out in my discussion of Ignatius's theology of martyrdom, the contrast in these texts is not between the authority of the apostles and that of Ignatius as a sub-apostolic bishop. The contrast is specifically between the apostles and Ignatius as a criminal according to Roman law. It is not a theological statement of two different types of authority but a sociological statement in which Ignatius, viewed from the vantage point of Roman society, carries no authority to command. The contrast is one of condition, not one of principled position. Thus, in the salutation of the *Letter to the Trallians* Ignatius does not necessarily mean by the phrase *en apostoliko characteri* "in an apostolic manner." The most natural rendering would be "in an apostolic stamp" or "with an apostolic stamp"

---

13 Walter Bauer p. 58.

(i.e. with an authority derived from the apostles). Such an interpretation accords well with Ignatius's emphasis on the bishops as having divine authorization and with the emphasis on apostolic succession found in 1 Clement 44.

In light of this, we can now understand Ignatius's conferral of blessing upon the church of Ephesus:

> If in a short amount of time I gained such fellowship with your bishop — a kind that is not human but spiritual — how much more do I *bless* you who are so mingled with him? As the church belongs to Jesus Christ, and as Jesus Christ belongs to the Father, that all may be harmonious in unity (Eph 5:1).

Like the term *character* in the salutation of *Trallians*, Ehrman and Holmes lessen the meaning of *makarizo* by choosing "congratulate" (Holmes) and "consider you fortunate" (Ehrman). In Christian Greek, *makarizo* is not simply a wish or congratulations. It connotes a blessing conferred, especially when spoken by a bishop. How could Ignatius confer a blessing on the Ephesians? It is because he saw his episcopal authority as founded on and derived from the apostles. He was not an apostle like Peter and Paul, to be sure, but his authority was apostolic. What is especially striking is that neither Ignatius nor Clement (cf. 1 Clem 44) speak of their views of authority as if they were new or novel. They believed the episcopal structure and authority of the church had been given them by the apostles.

The final phrase in the Ignatian letters relating to the structure of the church bears on Roman primacy. In the Salutation of the *Letter to the Romans* Ignatius employs two phrases that have generated much controversy. To understand their meaning, it is useful to quote the entire salutation:

> Ignatius, called Theophorus, to the church that receives mercy in the majesty of the Father Most High and of Jesus Christ his only Son. This church has been loved and enlightened in the will of him who willed all things that exist in accord with the faith and love of Jesus Christ, our God. *Your church presides in the region of the Romans*; it is worthy of God, worthy of propriety, worthy of blessing, worthy of praise, worthy of success, worthy of purity and *presiding in love*, named by Christ, named by the Father. I greet your church in the name of Jesus Christ, the Father's Son. To you who are united in flesh and spirit to his every command, filled with God's grace without distinction, and strained off from every foreign color, especially in Jesus Christ, our God, I give greetings blamelessly.

Ignatius's language is striking in that he ascribes to the church of Rome a special status which he does not give to any of the other churches in his letters. In addition to the two italicized phrases above, Ignatius engages in higher praise of this church than of any other. He lists nine attributes which set the Roman church apart from the others. Clearly, Ignatius holds the Roman church in high esteem. The differences of interpretation arise when the phrase "your church presides in the region of the Romans" is considered. This phrase *(hetis kai prokathetai in topo choriou Romaiou)* has been taken in several different ways, some of which tend to support the heightened status of the Roman church. Most Protestant interpretation has contended that this expression is just one more item of praise along with the other attributes mentioned by Ignatius and does not necessarily ascribe any special power to the church of Rome. They note that the phrase *en topo choriou Romaion* (lit. "in the place of the region of the Romans") simply means that this church rules in its own region as, for example, the church in Ephesus does in its respective region.[14] This interpretation then also sees the phrase "presiding in love " as Ignatius's way of praise for the generosity and love for the poor on the part of the Roman church rather than a statement of supremacy. Thus, these scholars see Ignatius as praising the church for its life rather than ascribing to it some governmental status over the other churches.

Everyone admits that the phrases used by Ignatius are passing comments which do not yield or presuppose a theology of Roman primacy. However, neither can it be denied that if Roman primacy was acknowledged this early within the church, the phrases used here by Ignatius are also consistent with that primacy. P.Th. Camelot notes that the text says "in the region of the Romans," not "over the region of the Romans." This implies that in the region where it is established, the church of Rome presides. But presides over what? The text does not say, but two possibilities immediately suggest themselves. First, the church of Rome is the presiding church in the Latin-speaking West or at least in the Italian peninsula. Second, the Roman church presides over the whole church. Whatever the answer, Camelot's comments seem justified: "It is difficult not to see in this text an allusion to a certain preeminence of the church of Rome over other regions."[15] Given that elsewhere the bishop is said to preside (*prokathemai*) in the place of God (e.g. Mag 6:1), it is likely that Ignatius has in mind a governmental connotation to the

---

14 Some Protestants have even tried to find some meaning of *prokathemai* other than "preside" but Schoedel seems to recognize this as a tendentious effort. See William R. Schoedel *Ignatius of Antioch* p. 166, n.4.

15 P.Th. Camelot *Ignace díAntioche. Polycarpe de Smyrne. Lettres. Martyre de Polycarpe*, p. 106.

same verb used here. And it is only a quibble to say that Ignatius speaks of the church and not the bishop of Rome. As he says elsewhere, the church is represented by the bishop and the bishop is manifested through the church. There can be no doubt that the claim to the primacy of the Roman church is consistent with the evidence in Ignatius's *Letter to the Romans.*

The church stands at the very center of the theology of Ignatius. The nature, structure, and mission of the church are all intimately intertwined. The church in his view is an organism which breathes the life given by God, which is nourished by the Eucharist, and whose structure derives from Christ through the apostles. The governmental structure of the church is not arbitrary, not simply a historical fact but grows out of the unity and harmony which Christ received from the Father and which he bestowed on his followers. That unity and harmony is found in the liturgy of the church and is expressed in the mutual love of its members. For Ignatius, the church stands at the very heart of reality.

Chapter Five
The Eucharist in the Theology of Ignatius

In the previous chapter we observed how the unity of the church was central to Ignatius's theology, and how that unity implied the holiness, catholicity, and apostolicity of the church. More importantly, we noted that in Ignatius's mind the unity of the church has its source in Christ's pastoral care of the church. The deeper source of unity is in God himself. That is why the Eucharist is so important for Ignatius. The Eucharist is the instrument through which the unity that is in God is communicated to the members of the church so they may be truly one.

Because Ignatius was writing occasional letters to the churches of Asia Minor, he does not address the subject of the Eucharist in any direct way, just as he does not address any major theological topic in a direct manner. However, by examining his passing comments on the Eucharist as reflections of his deeper theology, we come to see this mystery as intimately connected to other aspects of his thought. Ignatius mentions the Eucharist explicitly in three of his letters (*Letter to the*

Ephesians, Letter to the Philadelphians, and *Letter to the Smyrneans*) but there are clear eucharistic allusions in other letters such as the *Letter to the Romans.* The passages in the first three letters have to do with the liturgical celebration proper while other allusions are embedded within other aspects of Ignatius's theology. The relevant passages seem on the surface to be unproblematic, but the history of the study of Ignatius reveals quite disparate opinions of what Ignatius actually believed. Pierre Battifol has noted two opposing assessments of Ignatius's sacramental theology. The first claims that Ignatius believed in the Real Presence of Christ in the Eucharist; the other is that Ignatius saw the Eucharist in less realistic and more symbolic terms.[1] The latter conclusion seems rather odd given the realistic language that Ignatius uses. Let us carefully examine the context of Ignatius's eucharistic statements.

The theme of unity, so germane to Ignatius's theology, surfaces again in his references to the liturgy. The *Letter to the Philadelphians* seems especially concerned with the ravenous wolves which can tear the church apart (Philad 2:2). The answer to division and evil teaching (cf. 2:1) is to follow the shepherd appointed for the church. Schism must be consciously rejected by believers if they are to remain faithful to Christ. Avoiding schism can best be accomplished by liturgical unity and so Ignatius exhorts the Philadelphians,

> Therefore, be diligent to employ only one Eucharist. For there is [only] one flesh of our Lord Jesus Christ and there is [only] one cup for unity in his blood. There is one altar as there is one bishop together with the presbytery and the deacons, my fellow

[1] Pierre Battifol *L'Eucharistie: La Presence Réelle et la Transubstantiation* (Paris: Librairie Victor Lecoffre, 1913) 5th ed. p. 40 n.1.

servants. The purpose of all this is so that your practices will be
in accord with God's intention (Philad 4:1).

The structure of this exhortation is worth noting closely.
"Eucharist" (*eucharistia*) provides the overarching term for the
entire liturgy while the succeeding terms designate specific
parts of or actors in the liturgy (flesh, cup, altar, and bishop). In
each case the repetition of "one" leaves us in no doubt that
Ignatius is distinguishing between an aberrant, unauthorized
liturgy and a legitimate celebration under the authority of the
bishop. The emphasis on the "one flesh" and "one cup for unity
in his blood" reveals the deepest ground for Ignatius's idea of
the Eucharist. The "one flesh of our Lord Jesus Christ" evokes
the continuity between the historical Jesus and the liturgical
celebration of the church. The "one cup for unity in his blood"
is reminiscent of Paul's words in his letter to the Corinthians:

> is not the cup which we bless a participation in the blood of
> Christ? Is not the bread which we break a participation in the
> body of Christ? Because there is one bread, we who are many
> are one body because we all partake of the one bread (1 Cor
> 10:16,17).

Paul teaches that it is the body and blood of Christ which makes
the members of the church truly one. It is "because we all partake of the one loaf" that we become one body.

Ignatius draws on Paul's teaching and extends it into a new
situation that allows for a clear view of the meaning of the
eucharistic liturgy. Implied in the phrase "one flesh of our Lord
Jesus Christ" is the reality of the God-man Jesus. This becomes
evident if we ask in what sense many different churches with
different altars can all be said to be one. One answer might be
found in the symbolic actions of each church. If, for example,

all the churches of Asia Minor have the same liturgy, they are symbolically representing their unity. However, Ignatius places the emphasis elsewhere. His command to celebrate "one Eucharist" is based, not on a common liturgy, but on the "one flesh" of the real Incarnation. One can hear the docetic denials just below the surface. If, as the Docetists claimed, Christ only appeared to have taken on human flesh, and only appeared to have suffered, then the celebration of the Eucharist only appears to have his body too. In countering the virtual denial of Christ's humanity, Ignatius carefully chooses "one flesh" as the reason why unity is more than symbolic. The churches are one because they all ultimately have the same altar (the heavenly), the same bishop (Christ), and most of all the same nourishment (one flesh).

If the Docetists are just beneath the surface in Ignatius's exhortation in Philad 4:1, they are front and center in his condemnation of them in the *Letter to the Smyrneans* where the problem of unity and liturgy seems to have been quite acute:

> They abstain from the Eucharist and [appointed times] of prayer because they do not confess that the Eucharist is the flesh of our Savior Jesus Christ which suffered for our sins and which the Father in his kindness raised. Those who speak against God's gift will die in their disputes. It was better for them to love so they may be raised (Smyrn 7:1).

It is important not to read these lines with a modern mentality. The Docetists' abstention from the liturgy was more than a decision in favor of diversity of opinion and practice. They abstained from the authorized liturgy because they would not confess the faith of the church in the real humanity of Jesus in the Eucharist. When Ignatius says they abstained from prayer, he does not mean all prayer but public prayer with the church.[2] The refusal of the Docetists to pray with the church at the eucharistic feast was grounded in their denial of a true Incarnation.[3] Denial of the Incarnation leads to denial of the Real Presence of Christ in the Eucharist. If the eternal Word never truly became a man, how could his humanity be conveyed in the Eucharist? Yet we should not suppose that the Docetists necessarily denied any presence at all. Perhaps they even confessed Jesus's body in the sacrament. Their belief might be inferred from Ignatius's explanation of what they denied when he adds, "the flesh ... which suffered for our sins and which the Father in his kindness raised." They denied any identity between the historical body of Jesus and the eucharistic body.[4] Thus, it is impossible not to view Ignatius as

---

2   Almost all commentators on Ignatius agree on this point. Luke speaks in the same fashion in describing the day of Pentecost when he says that the new converts "devoted themselves to the apostles' teaching, to fellowship, to the breaking of bread, and to prayers" (Acts 2:42). The word "prayer" in Smyrn 7:1 may in fact refer to eucharistic prayer as we have indications that already this early in the church the celebration of the Eucharist was guided by set prayers as it is clearly in *Didache* 9: "Concerning the Eucharist, give thanks like this. First, the cup. We thank you, our Father, for the holy vine of David, your servant which you have made known to us through Jesus your servant. To you be glory forever," etc.

3   See Smyrn 3:1-3 for the extent of Ignatius's concern about the Docetists' denial of the Incarnation: "I know and believe that after the resurrection he [Christ] was in the flesh. And when he came to those around Peter, he said to them, 'Take, handle me, and see that I am not a bodiless demon.' And immediately they touched him and believed, once they were mingled with his flesh and blood. For this reason, they despised death and were found beyond death. And after the resurrection, he ate and drank with them as a fleshly man, although he was spiritually united with the Father."

4   The issue of whether the eucharistic body is the same as the historical body of Jesus which suffered and rose surfaced again in the Berengar controversy. Two extremes were avoided by the church. One was a denial of any continuity between the historical Jesus and the eucharistic Jesus; the other was a naive and

teaching the real human presence of Jesus Christ in the Eucharist.

What might overcome their denial of the Eucharist? The last two lines of the quotation from Smyrn 7:1 above speak of love. Denying God's gift leads to destruction; loving God and the church leads to resurrection. That is why Ignatius goes on to reaffirm that only the Eucharist authorized by the legitimate bishop is valid:

> You all should follow the bishop as Jesus Christ does the Father. Follow too the presbytery as the apostles, and honor the deacons as the command of God. Let no one do anything that is proper for the church without the bishop. Let that Eucharist be considered valid that is under the bishop or performed by one to whom he entrusts it (Smyrn 8:1).

Taken out of the wider context of Smyrn 7 or of the letters of Ignatius in general, this text might be interpreted as an attempt on Ignatius's part to exercise raw power and to assert the unchallenged authority of Polycarp as bishop of Smyrna. However, Ignatius is not opting for an authoritarian solution to heresy and schism. Rather, he is reminding the Smyrneans of where the true body and blood of Christ may be found because he seems to be aware of the dissidents' claims to have a valid Eucharist. The underlying question is where to find Jesus Christ and that question amounts to asking where a valid Eucharist may be found. This reasoning makes sense of the famous words that follow:

> Wherever the bishop appears, let there be the fullness [of the church] as wherever Christ Jesus appears, there is the catholic

---

crude identification of the two. The ultimate answer embraced by the church was the notion of a substantial identity. While Jesus's accidents (hair, skin, etc.) are not present in the Eucharist, the substance of his humanity is present.

church. It is not lawful to baptize or to hold an agape feast without the bishop. On the other hand, what he approves is pleasing to God so that everything that is practiced may be certain and valid (Smyrn 8:2).

We examined these words carefully in the previous chapter but here we can now see their relevance to the sacramental issue at stake in Ignatius's letters. The bishop represents Christ to the church, and the liturgy he authorizes is the place where Christ can be found. It is not enough to have any Eucharist. One must have *the* valid Eucharist in order to have Jesus Christ and the catholic church.

The last eucharistic text I wish to consider is the famous expression "the medicine of immortality" from the *Letter to the Ephesians*, chapter 20:

> If Jesus Christ counts me worthy by your prayer, and it is his will, in a second treatise that I am about to write, I will show you the plan which I began leading to the new man, Jesus Christ in his faith, and in his love, in his suffering, and resurrection. (2) This is especially the case if the Lord shows me that each of you gathers together in one faith and in one Jesus Christ who came from the stock of David in the flesh, the Son of Man and Son of God. This results in you obeying your bishop and your presbytery with an undistracted mind as you break bread which is the medicine of immortality, the antidote against death and life forever through Jesus Christ (Eph 20:1,2).

Ignatius's phrase "the medicine of immortality" (*athanasias pharmakon*) emphasizes the connection between the celebration of the Eucharist and the salvation Christ wrought through his humanity. Again it is evident how unity of doctrine, obedience to the bishop, and sacramental communion are inextricably intertwined. In Eph 20 these connections show up as "gathering in one faith," obeying the bishop, and presbyters and "breaking one bread." Ignatius uses the Lucan language of "breaking bread" to show an affinity with the churches founded by Paul (cf. Acts 20:7). That the expression refers to the Eucharist is clear from the attribution which follows. The breaking of bread is a "medicine of immortality" that gives nothing less than "an antidote against death" and "constant life in Jesus Christ." Such extravagant claims for such a simple celebration no doubt depend on another contextual factor. Ignatius mentions faith in Jesus Christ and immediately adds that he is the one who is "from the stock of David in the flesh" (i.e. his human nature) glossing the phrase from Romans 1:3 describing Jesus as "the son of man and the son of God." Here we have hints of what we shall see later in the fathers, that the union of humanity and divinity in Jesus Christ brings eternal life to the recipients of sacramental communion. The power of the eucharistic bread to convey eternal life is rooted in the fact that the Eucharist is "the flesh of our Savior Jesus Christ" (Smyrn 7:1). If the eucharistic elements *are* the humanity of Christ, and if this humanity is forever joined with the divinity of Christ, then it follows that the Eucharist imparts an "antidote against death" by granting "continual life in Christ."

While the connection between the Eucharist and eternal life is not unusual, the metaphor "medicine of immortality" is unique at this stage of history. Ignatius's choice of terminology grows out of his earlier mention of Christ as the divine physician:

> There is one physician, both fleshly and spiritual, born and unborn becoming God in the flesh, true life in death, from

> Mary and from God, at first suffering then incapable of suffering. This is Jesus Christ our Lord (Eph 7:2).

Like so many of the later fathers, Ignatius revels in the paradoxes that he can ascribe to the gospel. The union of those opposites makes Jesus Christ unique and indicates his power to convey immortality — an abstract, divine quality — through a tangible means — bread and medicine. The union of opposites is the best way to understand the phrase "medicine of immortality." It should strike the reader as strange and arresting, just as the list of opposites in Eph 7:2 evokes surprise. How could a medicine give immortality? It is because the physician who gives the medicine is himself immortal, and also conveys himself in the medicine. For Ignatius, Christ is both physician and medicine just as he is also both priest and victim.

Chapter Six
Polycarp of Smyrna: Life, Martyrdom, and Writing

In contrast to how little we actually know about the life of Ignatius of Antioch, there exists an abundance of material on the life of Polycarp of Smyrna. We have Ignatius's *Letter to Polycarp* and the later *Martyrdom of Polycarp* in addition to what can be inferred from Polycarp's own *Letter to the Philippians*. Irenaeus, the late second century bishop of Lyons, as a boy heard Polycarp preach in Smyrna. Writing years later (ca. A.D. 190) from ancient Gaul (France), Irenaeus left remembrances of Polycarp which fit into the whole picture of this famous martyr of Asia Minor.

In a letter preserved by Eusebius in his fourth century *Ecclesiastical History*, Irenaeus wrote to his childhood friend Florinus, who in his later years had turned to the Gnostic heresies that the bishop of Lyons fought against so vigorously. Irenaeus attempted to persuade his old friend Florinus to abandon his new views by appealing to the antiquity and orthodoxy of Polycarp, their common teacher. In the course of his appeal we learn about Polycarp's episcopal ministry at Smyrna:

> When I was a boy, I saw you in lower Asia with Polycarp, acting splendidly in the royal hall, and endeavoring to be highly thought of by him. I recall the events of that time more clearly than those of recent years. For the things you learn in childhood grow in the soul, and are united with it; I am able to describe the very place in which the blessed Polycarp sat as he discoursed, his goings and his comings, the character of his life, his physical appearance, his speeches to the multitudes, and the accounts which he gave of his interactions with John and with the others who had seen the Lord. I also recall when he remembered their words, and what he heard from them concerning the Lord, concerning his miracles and teaching. What Polycarp received then from eyewitnesses of the Word of life, he related in its entirety in harmony with the Scriptures. By the mercy of God, I listened to these things attentively, noting them down, not on paper, but in my heart. By the grace of God I always recall them faithfully. And I am able to bear witness before God that if that blessed and apostolic presbyter had heard any such thing, he would have cried out, and stopped his ears, according to his custom. He would have exclaimed, "O good God, unto what times have you preserved me that I should have to endure these things? And he would have fled from the place where, sitting or standing, he had heard such words. And this can be shown plainly from the letters that he sent, either to the neighboring churches strengthening them, or to some of the brethren admonishing and exhorting them. This can be plainly seen.[1]

All the information we possess about Polycarp's life must be woven together into a coherent narrative to arrive at a reliable picture.[2] According to Irenaeus, Polycarp was not only a

---

1 Eusebius *Ecclesiastical History* bk 5 ch.20 sec. 5-8.

2 I will not rely here on the *Life of Polycarp* (*Vita Polycarpi*) written by a certain Pionius. The work is of questionable historical value since it probably dates from

disciple of John and friends with others who had seen Jesus on earth, he was appointed by the apostles as the bishop of Smyrna. Tertullian specifies that the appointment was accomplished by none other than John the apostle himself.[3] Polycarp, of course, was the bishop of Smyrna when Ignatius passed through en route to Rome around the year A.D. 110. If we suppose that the apostle John died some time in the last decade of the first century and that Polycarp was in fact ordained and appointed by John, he most likely assumed the episcopal office no later than 95 and possibly as early as 85. Even assuming his young age at ordination, it is unlikely that he would have been consecrated a bishop if he were under twenty-five years of age. This would put his birth some time between the years 60-70, which means that he was between thirty and forty years old in 110 when Ignatius visited Smyrna. If Polycarp was indeed eighty-six years old when he was martyred, as the *Martyrdom of Polycarp* implies,[4] this would mean that the martyrdom took place A.D. 146 to 156.

The *Martyrdom* itself does not tell us the year of Polycarp's demise; it only specifies the day, 23 February. Many scholars have dated the martyrdom 23 February 155. However, if the information provided by Eusebius on Polycarp's visit to Anicetus in Rome is reliable, Polycarp must have been in Rome no earlier than 154/155. Anicetus died in either 165 or 166. Perhaps the best we can estimate is that Polycarp was

the fourth century. The text of this work can be found in Lightfoot *The Apostolic Fathers*. However, the *Martyrdom of Polycarp* translated here probably dates from the early third century.

3 "For this is the manner in which the apostolic churches transmit their registers: as the church of Smyrna, which records that Polycarp was placed therein by John." Tertullian *On Prescription Against Heretics* bk 32.

4 In the *Martyrdom* (ch.9) Polycarp says only that he has served Christ eighty-six years. This may refer to his age or to the time since his baptism. If he was baptized as an infant, it would not make much difference.

martyred in Smyrna during the dates of Anicetus's papacy (154/155 to 165/166).[5] One thing is certain, all the information we possess about Polycarp lauds him as a stellar exemplar of Christian faith, life, and death. Greek-speaking Christians, no doubt aware of the meaning of his name — *Polycarpos* means "much fruit" — drew deep and lasting inspiration from the account of the manner of his death in the famous *Martyrdom of Polycarp* to which we now turn.

The Teaching of the *Martyrdom of Polycarp*[6]

More important than the date of Polycarp's death is the teaching about Christian martyrdom that the document contains. A careful reading reveals that the author wanted not only to recount the circumstances of Polycarp's death but also to instruct Christians on how one should prepare for death. Much like the canonical gospels themselves, the author of the *Martyrdom* uses historical narrative

---

5   "and when the blessed Polycarp was at Rome in the time of Anicetus, and they disagreed a little about certain other things, they immediately made peace with one another, not caring to quarrel over this matter [the date of Easter]. For neither could Anicetus persuade Polycarp not to observe what he had always observed with John the disciple of our Lord, and the other apostles with whom he had associated; nor could Polycarp persuade Anicetus to observe it as he said that he ought to follow the customs of the presbyters that had preceded him." Eusebius *Ecclesiastical History* bk 4 ch.14.

6   The complete text of the *Martyrdom* is difficult to establish with certainty. The biggest problem has to do with the ending because there are two textual traditions. Chapter 21 of the *Martyrdom* consists of a kind of historical appendix situating Polycarp's death in the Greek calendar. Then chapter 22 has two different forms, both of which are translated here. The shorter version (see version 1) is thought to be an appendix added by the Church in Philomelium, and probably originates from before the 4th century. The second appendix (the so-called Moscow manuscript) is longer and was probably composed at the end of the fourth century.

for pedagogical purposes.

The *Martyrdom of Polycarp* is written as a letter from the church of Smyrna to the church of Philomelium but is clearly meant for all Christendom.[7] The author wishes to portray Polycarp's death as a witness — *martus* in Greek means witness — to the gospel of Jesus Christ which counts earthly life as a prelude to eternal life. In the author's estimation, a Christian martyrdom benefits not only the martyr himself but all who wish to imitate Christ (1:2). Throughout the *Martyrdom* we find parallels between the death of Jesus and that of Polycarp. Chapter 8 says that Polycarp prayed in the manner of Jesus's prayer for his disciples (see Jn 17) and that he was led into the city of Smyrna on a donkey. The day was a "great Sabbath."

The didactic character of the *Martyrdom* becomes clear with the contrastive example of a certain Phrygian named Quintus who offered himself for martyrdom. His failure to follow through revealed that his actions were not in accord with the gospel (4:1). Polycarp's arrest and execution, by contrast, were forced upon him. We are told that a certain Germanicus was to be martyred first but the crowd called for Polycarp in his place. After Polycarp heard of his impending arrest, his faithful people urged him to flee to a country house where he could be hid from authorities (5:1). While praying there, Polycarp had a vision of being burned alive within three days.

What is striking about the *Martyrdom of Polycarp* is that the author does not portray the Roman officials as monsters or bloodthirsty tyrants. Given the Roman persecution of the Christians, the author might understandably have painted a

---

7 "to all those sojourners of the holy and catholic church in every place" Mart Polyc Sal.

picture of domination and tyranny, but his descriptions pursue another tack. The proconsul of Asia, Statius Quadratus, is shown as a man of some compassion, who attempts to persuade the accused that sacrificing to Caesar is a simple matter of conformity with the law. It is precisely the apparently tolerant attitude on the part of Roman officials which makes the Christian attitude of Polycarp stand out in bolder relief.

Polycarp says that swearing an oath of allegiance to Caesar and sacrificing to the emperor is tantamount to denying Christ as king of all. Strengthened by a voice from heaven (9:1), Polycarp asked the inevitable and decisive question, "I have served him eight-six years and he has done me no wrong. How can I blaspheme my King who saved me?" With this gesture, needlessly defiant from the Roman point of view, Polycarp is prepared for execution. Brought to the fire for his incineration, the holy bishop reminds himself and others that there is an eternal fire waiting those who are ungodly (11:2). The uncontrollable rage that issues forth from the crowd of pagans and Jews is without a doubt due to this man being "the father of Christians." By destroying Polycarp, the crowd hoped to silence the Christians and to stop their progress within Smyrna. But Polycarp went willingly to his execution by fire. We are told that he did not need to be bound by nails because God gave him the stamina to remain in the fire. Before his demise, Polycarp offers a prayer in imitation of Jesus praying on the cross. We will look at the prayer in more detail presently. Since the flames could not extinguish his life, the executioner thrust a dagger into the side of the father of Christians, signaling yet another parallel with the death of Jesus (see Jn 19:34).

The author concludes his account by distinguishing between the worship of Christ himself as the dying Messiah and the veneration of martyrs (17,1,2) probably because the pagans could not distinguish between the two kinds of death. Martyrdom then is seen as the ultimate imitation of Christ and the highest means of partaking of his grace and life.

The Prayer of Polycarp

One particular section (chapter 14) of the *Martyrdom* has drawn special attention because it contains a prayer of Polycarp before his death, a section replete with liturgical overtones. This prayer, so full of biblical language, expresses the true spirit of martyrdom in ancient Christianity.[8] Here Polycarp blesses God for having:

> thought me worthy of this day and this hour to be numbered among your martyrs in the cup of your Christ, for the resurrection of eternal life, of both soul and body, in the incorruptibility of the Holy Spirit. Among these may I be received today before you, in the sacrifice that is rich and acceptable.

Like other early liturgical prayers that have come down to us, Polycarp's request "to be numbered among your martyrs" hearkens back to those early Saints who, upon their deaths, fully partook of eternal life and experienced the incorruptibility given through the fullness of the Holy Spirit's indwelling. The phrase "in the cup (chalice) of your Christ" points both to the liturgical practice of the church on earth and to the death of Jesus which is embodied in that eucharistic cup.

---

8 I hereby gratefully acknowledge my dependence on the excellent exposition of this prayer by Camelot. See P.Th. Camelot, *Ignace d'Antioche. Polycarpe de Smyrne. Lettres. Martyre de Polycarpe*, 4th ed. *Sources chrétiennes* 10. (Paris: Editions du Cerf, 1969) pp. 202-207.

Like most of the liturgical prayers of Christian antiquity, Polycarp's prayer is trinitarian to the core but its focus lies in the address to the Father. He is "the Almighty" (*Pantokrator*), the God of angels and (heavenly) powers and of all creation. God "the Almighty One" translates *YHWH Sabaoth* or *YHWH Shaddai* used in the Old Testament. It is the language used in the book of Revelation to describe the praises of those in the heavenly court. Particularly striking is Revelation 4:8 where the four living creatures cry out, "Holy, holy, holy, Lord God Almighty, who was, and is, and is to come."[9] The cry in Revelation is clearly modeled on Isaiah 6:3, "Holy, holy, holy, Lord God of Sabaoth. The whole earth is full of his glory." The author of the Apocalypse has altered the Hebrew text of Isaiah to focus not on the manifestation of God's glory but on the eternal nature of God who was and is and is to come. Polycarp's address to the Father as the Almighty may very well have derived from a liturgical use of the book of Revelation in his church at Smyrna. In any case, it reflects the early Christian idea that all prayer is ultimately directed to the same source of life and redemption that is at the same time the goal of the Christian pilgrimage, the Father Almighty. It is appropriately used by Polycarp as he readies himself for his final journey back to the Father whom he has served on earth.

Polycarp would not, however, be a *Christian* martyr without that "beloved and blessed child Jesus Christ" (Mart Polyc 14:1), because it is only through Christ that "we have received knowledge of you" (i.e. the Father). Polycarp's language at the beginning of his prayer draws on a prominent theme in the NT, especially developed in the Gospel of John. In

---

9   For other uses of *Pantokrator* (Almighty) in Revelation, see Rev 1:8; 11:17; 15:3; 16:7; 21:22.

response to Thomas's request to know the way he is about to go, Jesus responds, "I am the way, the truth, and the life. No one comes to the Father except through me. If you knew me, you would have known my Father. From now on, you know him and have seen him" (Jn 14:6,7). When Philip follows up by asking to be shown the Father, Jesus responds with a penetrating question, "So great a time I have been with you and you do not know me, Philip? He who has seen me has seen the Father" (Jn 14:8,9).[10] By using the word "child" (*pais*), Polycarp expresses the fundamental Christian assumption that knowledge of God the Father comes through Jesus Christ.

Pais is used of Jesus in the speeches in Acts 3:13,26 (by Peter) and in 4:27,30 (in the prayer of the Jerusalem church). It means a small child, even an infant, though at times it is applied to "servants." In this latter sense we see it used in Matthew 12:18 in a quotation from Isaiah 42:1. It is also used in the prayers of the *Didache* (9:3; 10:2,3) and may well have become a preferred term in early Christian liturgical prayers. In such a context, it may have expressed both sides of its range of meaning. Jesus as "the beloved and blessed child" of the Father has come as his servant to reveal the fullness of the Father. Camelot summarized the significance of *pais* in the Bible and in the early Christian use of this term:

> Thus, in ritual terms fixed by the tradition of the Old Testament and by liturgical use, *pais* expresses a theology older perhaps but very firm in its formulations. Jesus is the "servant" of Yahweh, fulfilling in his person the prophecy of Isaiah but this servant is not a slave (*doulos*) as a creature would be. He is the "child," the well-loved and unique Son.

---

10 Mt 11:25-30 contains another expression of Jesus's unique revelation of the Father.

God is the Father of his well-loved and blessed child, Jesus Christ.[11]

As noted above, this prayer contains many liturgical connections that carry theological overtones. It does not seem likely that Polycarp's prayer was some standard form used in liturgy or by Christians generally. We have no way of knowing just how unique this prayer may be. However, it should not surprise us that a bishop of the church in the second century would weave together liturgical references into his personal prayer at the hour of his death. If he had spent the greater part of his eighty-six years praying a particular liturgy, perhaps with some variations, the content of those prayers would most likely have been ingrained into his mind and heart, just as his *Letter to the Philippians* contains numerous references to the NT because he had those texts embedded in his memory.

The framing of the prayer suggests a liturgical origin. In imitation of Jesus, who looked up into heaven in prayer,[12] Polycarp was "looking up into heaven." This posture may have been standard for a presbyter celebrating the liturgy in the second century (the *orans* position). Then Polycarp refers to the eucharistic "cup of your Christ" and later to "the eternal and heavenly high priest Jesus Christ." He concludes with a phrase that would become usual fare in ending liturgical prayers ("Through him and with him in the Holy Spirit be glory to you now and forevermore. Amen"). The words "the

---

11 P.Th. Camelot *Ignace d'Antioche. Polycarpe de Smyrne. Lettres. Martyre de Polycarpe*, 4th ed. *Sources chrétiennes* 10. (Paris: Éditions du Cerf, 1969) pp. 205.

12 Of the 25 instances of *anablepo* ("look up") in the NT, Jesus is the subject in four cases. In three of these cases, *anablepo* occurs in the story of the blessing of the loaves and fish (Mt 14:19; Mk 6:41; Lk 9:16). In the fourth (Mk 7:34), Jesus looks up before healing the mute and deaf man.

cup of your Christ" point to the inner meaning of martyrdom. The cup of suffering that Polycarp embraces unites him
with the Eucharist, the substance of which is the suffering of
Christ for the world. It is this union, rather than a sheer act
of the human will, that allows him to become "a rich and
acceptable sacrifice."

Another reason for believing that Polycarp's prayer contains liturgical echoes is its parallels with the *Didache*. Almost
all scholars of the *Didache* agree that it was probably written
before 120 and therefore predates Polycarp's martyrdom.
The prescribed liturgical prayers (chs. 9, 10, 14) in the
Didache belie the notion that worship in the early church was
free-flowing and spontaneous. Although it is impossible to say
how close the liturgy used in Smyrna was to that used in Syria
— the probable origin of the *Didache* — the parallels suggest
that there was some uniformity in liturgy across the church.
Polycarp's use of *pais*, discussed above, is found in the *Didache*
as well: "We thank you, our Father, for the holy vine of David
your servant (*pais*) which you have made known to us through
Jesus your servant (*pais*)."[13] The verb of knowing in this
prayer finds a place in Polycarp's prayer as well, "Through
him we have received knowledge of you" (Mart Polyc 14:1). It
would seem that liturgical prayers of both Syria and Asia
Minor stressed the sonship and servanthood of Jesus as the
unique channel through which knowledge of the Father was
revealed. Polycarp, realizing that he was at the end of his
earthly journey, spontaneously drew on ideas found in the
liturgy that he had prayed for his entire episcopal ministry.

---

13 *Didache* 9. This prayer is used twice, once for the cup and once for the bread.

The Letter to the Philippians[14]

The only writing from the pen of Polycarp is his *Letter to the Philippians*, though some indications are that he wrote other letters that have not survived. This letter has been viewed as simple and uninteresting by some scholars while others have found it significant for understanding the context and content of Polycarp's theology. At first sight, the letter appears to contain somewhat random exhortations on both theological and moral topics. Unlike most of Paul's letters in the New Testament, it does not seem to be addressing any pressing problems in the church at Philippi. In chapter thirteen, we are told in fact that the letter was attached to several letters of Ignatius that the Philippians had requested of Polycarp. Thus, *The Letter to the Philippians* has the appearance of a cover letter for the collection sent to Philippi. In chapter thirteen, we hear Polycarp informing the Philippians of his intention to fulfill Ignatius's request to forward letters on to Syrian Antioch.[15]

A closer reading of the letter, however, indicates that Polycarp has several other, more substantial purposes in writing it. One is that he wants to encourage and warn the Philippians about the disorder fomented by the presbyter Valens and his wife who have been lured by the love of money. Several times in the letter Polycarp reminds them that the love of money can be the root or foundation of many evils

---

14 The text of the letter survives in nine Greek manuscripts but all break off in chapter nine, verse 2. Chapters ten through fourteen are preserved only in a Latin translation while chapter 13 (in Greek) is quoted by Eusebius in his *Ecclesiastical History* of the fourth century.

15 "You and Ignatius wrote to me that if anyone departs for Syria, he should carry along the letters from you. I myself will do this if I have a suitable opportunity, or [send] someone who is an ambassador for you." Phil Polyc 13:1,

(see 4:1). The second motif is Polycarp's concern about theological deviation. His repeated emphasis on the death and resurrection of Christ seems to arise out of a lingering Docetism that was evident in Ignatius's letters and earlier in 1 John. The root cause of Docetism is the denial that Jesus Christ has come in the flesh (7:1). Polycarp is convinced that the down-to-earth reality of the Christian life is based on the historical truth of the Incarnation of the Son of God and his accomplishment of redemption through his death and resurrection (Paschal Mystery).

The last striking feature of this letter, and the one Polycarp mentions the most, deals with the challenge of moral living. Here Polycarp shows his awareness of his pastoral duty not only to his own church at Smyrna but to the larger church as well. Like many bishops before and after him, he was well aware that not all members of the church could adjudicate finely tuned theological points but all could be expected to pursue faith, hope, and love in imitation of Christ. And so he opens his letter with an expression of joy in the Philippians's right living (ch 1). Then follow abundant exhortations that draw on numerous NT texts in which Polycarp expands on the scriptural texts.[16] Of all the moral dangers of which Polycarp warns his readers, he identifies the love of money (*philarguria*) as the source of all moral problems (see 4:1-3; 5:2; 6:1). He contrasts greed with the greatest virtue of justice or righteousness (*dikaiosune*).[17] If we use the

---

16 For the latest exploration of Polycarp's use of NT texts, especially Paul, see Kenneth Berding, *Polycarp and Paul: An Analysis of their Literary & Theological Relationship in light of Polycarp's Use of Biblical and Extra-Biblical Literature* (Leiden: Brill, 2002).

17 *dikaiosune* illustrates different traditions of translation. Protestant scholars, following traditional English versions, tend to use "righteousness" while Catholic scholars, following the Vulgate tradition, have tended to use "justice" (cf. Latin *justitia*).

rest of Polycarp's moral exhortations to give content to this *dikaiosune*, we can conclude that for the bishop of Smyrna, a just life is one that spans a wide range of other virtues.

The picture of Polycarp painted by our various sources of information is of a man who was a faithful shepherd of the church in Smyrna. His concern for his flock and for the whole church is reflected in his desire to see the members of the church live according to the gospel. To be faithful to Christ and his gospel meant above all living in holiness and justice (*dikaiosune*). Such living would be the characteristic of a good citizen (*politeuomai*) even if the Greco-Roman world did not recognize it as such. More than anything, the Christian must be ready to give his or her life as an offering to God in martyrdom. That, of course, is Polycarp's greatest virtue. His life was crowned with a sacrificial death, the culmination of his existence as Christian and as bishop.

Translations and
Commentaries

Chapter Seven
Ignatius's Letter to the Ephesians
Translation and Commentary

Ignatius's *Letter to the Ephesians* is his longest (21 chapters) and deals with a variety of subjects. We possess two previous letters to this church: Paul's *Letter to the Ephesians* and John the Seer's *Letter to the Ephesians* in the book of Revelation (Rev 2:1-6). Both are found in the New Testament. We know more from the New Testament about Ephesus than about any other of the cities, besides Rome, to which Ignatius addressed his letters. Acts 19 recounts the apostle Paul's ministry among and confrontation with the Ephesians. Ephesus was a large and productive commercial center whose religious life centered around the worship of Artemis (Diana). We learn from this letter that Onesimus was the bishop of Ephesus in Ignatius's day (1:2). As in all his other letters, Ignatius urges these Christians to be in unity with their bishop (e.g. 4:2) because the Docetists were denying the true humanity of Christ (7:2; 10:2; 16:1,2; 18:2; 19:1; 20:2). We also find here the unique emphasis on Jesus Christ as the one physician (7:2) and the Eucharist as "the medicine of immortality" (20:2).

Salutation[1]

Ignatius, also called Theophorus,[2] writes to the church at Ephesus in Asia [Minor], most worthy of all blessing, greetings in the great fullness of God the Father, and especially in Jesus Christ and in blameless joy. To the church that was marked out before all ages to be constantly oriented to an enduring glory, a glory united unchangeably and chosen in true suffering in the will of the Father and of Jesus Christ, our God.[3]

Chapter 1

(1) Since in God I received the much loved name[4] that you purchased by a just nature in accord with the faith and love in Christ Jesus, our Savior, and since as imitators of God you rekindled [yourselves] in

---

1   Ignatius's letter follows the standard form of ancient Greek letters: so-and-so to so-and-so, greetings. Writers would often note praiseworthy characteristics of the addressees as Ignatius does here.

2   The name Theophorus means "God-bearer." Several times in these letters Ignatius uses the language of participation in the divine life. See Eph 4:2; 8:1, and Magn 14:1, "filled with God."

3   In this opening salutation Ignatius highlights the paradoxical position of the church in the world. It is destined for "enduring glory" but this high calling is lived out in the "true sufferings" of Christ in the world. Later fathers will speak of Christ suffering in and through the members of the church. St. Cyprian of Carthage speaks of Christ as the example of suffering for the Christian (Epistle 6) and St. Augustine speaks of the head of the church, Christ, suffering through Christians who comprise the body (*Commentary on Psalm* 61:4).

4   See Rev 2:3, "You have patience and have borne much for my name."

the blood of God,[5] you perfectly completed the work of our family.[6]
(2) When you heard that I had been brought bound from
Syria[7] for the sake of the common name and hope, and that
I had hoped, by your prayer, to obtain the privilege of doing
battle with beasts in Rome[8] and so be a disciple, you were
diligent to see me.[9] (3) Since I have received your full congregation in God's name in the person of Onesimus,[10] your
bishop in the flesh whose love is beyond words. It is him I ask
you to love in accord with Jesus Christ as well as all of you trying to be like him. Blessed is He who graciously gave you such
a one as a bishop!

---

5   "the blood of God," an unusual expression, is used only here by Ignatius. He
    normally uses "blood of Christ" (Smyrn 6:1; Trall 8:1). While "blood of God" is
    unusual, it fits with Ignatius's belief that Jesus Christ is God (see the end of the
    salutation above) and therefore that the union of divinity and humanity in Christ
    allows us to transfer ideas to his divinity which strictly speaking belong to his
    humanity. Christ is *one* person with two natures.The pairing of "blood of God"
    with the verb "rekindle" and "family work" suggests that the Eucharist contains
    an empowering fire to do the work of God in the church.

6   More lit. this sentence could be translated, "you rekindled in the blood of God
    the work of our family; you perfectly completed it."

7   Ignatius usually refers to his own church by the region (Syria) rather than by the
    city (Antioch).

8   *theriomacheo* ("to battle beasts") may have a special significance for the Ephesian
    Christians because Paul tells us that he fought with beasts in Ephesus. In 1 Cor
    15:32, Paul says, "If I did battle with beasts in Ephesus according to man, what
    profit is that to me?" Ignatius may be calling this to their attention because Paul's
    bravery was widely remembered.

9   The last phrases of this verse could also be translated, "you were diligent to see
    that I may be able to obtain being a true disciple."

10 This Onesimus is probably not the same as mentioned by Paul as Philemon's
    slave (see Philem 1:10).

Chapter 2

(1) Now about my fellow slave,[11] Burrhus who is your blessed deacon in every way by God's will,[12] I ask that he remain for your honor and that of your bishop. And Crocus, who is worthy of God and of you, has refreshed me in every way; I received him as an exemplar of your love. In the same way may the Father of Jesus Christ refresh him together with Onesimus, Burrhus, Euplus, and Fronto. Through them I have seen you all in love. (2) May I enjoy you always if in fact I am worthy of you. It is fitting in every way to glorify Jesus Christ who has glorified you so that, knit together in a single obedience, you may be holy in every respect by being subject to the bishop and to the presbytery.[13]

Chapter 3

(1) I do not command you as if I were someone.[14] Since I

---

11 "fellow slave." I have chosen to translate *doulos* and its compounds (*sundoulos*) as "slave" to distinguish it from *diakonos* "deacon." Both words can be translated as "servant" but Ignatius always uses *diakonos* as a designation for the office of deacon. Paul often calls himself a *doulos* in the salutations of his letters (see e.g. Paul in Rom 1:1).

12 *kata theon* ("by God's will," lit. "according to God"). Ehrmann takes this phrase as a personal attribute of Burrhus ("your godly deacon"). Either translation is possible. *Kata theon* is used by Paul (see e.g. Rom 8:27). Given Ignatius's emphasis elsewhere on the divine authority behind church offices, "by God's will" seems to fit his theology well.

13 "presbytery" means the body of elders. It is used three times in the NT. Paul's use of *presbuterion* in 1 Tim 4:14 shows that the body of presbyters was involved in the ordination of new presbyters. Later presbyters would be called priests. Today priests are still called presbyters and the body of priests in a diocese is called the presbyterate.

14 Ignatius uses here as elsewhere the form of humble appeal to his fellow believers by acknowledging his need for their help in facing his future martyrdom in Rome.

am in chains in that name [of Christ], I am not yet complete in Jesus Christ. For now I am just at the beginning of being a disciple and I speak to you as fellow learners. I must be anointed[15] by you with faith, instruction, endurance, patience. (2) But your love does not permit me to keep silent about you. So I take the opportunity in advance to encourage you so you will agree[16] with the will of God. For Jesus Christ, our common[17] life, is the will of the Father as also the bishops, who are appointed in various regions, are in the will of Jesus Christ.[18]

Chapter 4

(1) Therefore, it is fitting that you agree with the opinion (or will) of the bishop as you are doing. Your rightly famous presbytery is worthy of God. It is in harmony with the bishop like strings tuned to a harp. For this reason, Jesus Christ is praised in your harmony and in your united love.[19] (2) Now,

---

15 *hupaleiphtheinai* ("anointed"). Ehrman ("be prepared by you") and Holmes ("be trained by you") flatten the metaphor in their translations. I have chosen to keep it because Ignatius is referring to a practice among the Greeks of anointing, or better rubbing, an athlete's body with oil to prepare him for a wrestling match. He must prepare for his martyrdom with the virtues of faith, etc. His request grows out of his view that members of the church share the grace of God with one another through empathetic prayer and sacrifice. Paul also used athletic metaphors (cf. 2 Tim 2:5) to describe his own impending martyrdom and later Greek fathers will do the same.

16 "Agree with" is lit. "run with" (*suntrechete*), i.e. to live in harmony.

17 *adiakriton* ("common life"). Ehrman has "Jesus Christ, who cannot be distinguished from our life."

18 I detect in Ehrman's translation "the bishops .... share the mind of Jesus Christ" a slightly softer note than my translation, which is more literal.

19 Ignatius shows how obedience to proper authority and love for fellow Christians go hand in hand. Seeking unity with the whole church requires "running with the will of the bishop" and the presbytery (priests). This harmony in doctrine and affection brings praise to Jesus Christ. Ignatius follows Paul's teachings on unity within the church. The apostle urges Christians to be united in mind and

each of you, become a chorus together so that by a united voice in harmony as you take up the tune of God in unity, you may sing in one voice through Jesus Christ to the Father. This is so that the Father may hear and recognize you by the good things you do, you who are members of his Son.[20] So, it is useful for you to be in blameless unity that you may always partake of God.[21]

Chapter 5

(1) If in a short amount of time I gained such fellowship with your bishop — a kind that is not human but spiritual — how much more do I bless[22] you who are so mingled with him? As the church belongs to[23] Jesus Christ, and as Jesus Christ belongs to the Father, that all may be harmonious in unity.

---

heart (see 1 Cor 1:10-17 and Phil 2:1ff) in obedience to Jesus's prayer in John chapter 17, "that all may be one as you, Father, are in me and I in you that they may be one that the world may know that you sent me" (Jn 17:21).

20 The unity Ignatius enjoins here flows from "being members of his Son." To be a true member of the church in harmony means belonging to Christ. Ignatius again follows Paul's doctrine of the church in which Christ is the head of the body and individual believers are members of Christ's body (see 1 Cor 12:12,19,20,27 and Eph 5:23).

21 Here Ignatius expresses two themes that will echo down through the centuries. First, singing through Jesus Christ to the Father means that Christ is the leader of praise to the Father. The liturgy the church engages on earth enters into the heavenly praise through the Son. Among others, John Chrysostom and Germanos of Constantinople will emphasize this point. Second, partaking of God means sharing in the life of the triune God. Later Greek fathers use the same word as here (*metecho*), as well as sharing (*koinoneo*) and receiving (*metalambano*).

22 *makarizo* ("bless you"). Holmes's choice of "congratulate" is too weak as is Ehrman's "consider you fortunate." In Christian Greek, *makarizo* is not simply a wish or congratulations. It connotes a blessing conferred, especially when spoken by a bishop.

23 I read the dative case as a dative of possession.

(2) Let no one deceive you. Unless someone is inside the sanctuary,[24] he does not have the bread of God. If the prayer of one or two has such great power, how much more does the prayer of the bishop and the whole church?[25] (3) He who does not come together in unity is proud and has judged himself for it is written, "God opposes the proud."[26] So let us be diligent not to oppose the bishop that we may be subject to God.

Chapter 6

(1) When someone sees the bishop being silent, that much more should he revere him. Everyone that the steward sends to look after his own stewardship we should receive as being like him who sent him. So it is clear with respect to the bishop that we should view him as the Lord himself.[27] (2) So Onesimus himself highly praises your good order in God because you all live in accord with truth and because no heresy[28] lives in your

---

24 *thusiasterion* ("sanctuary") normally means "altar" in Christian Greek, though most translators choose "sanctuary" because it sounds strange to say "inside the altar." Ignatius refers to the liturgy of the church where the bread of God can only be found on the altar on which the Eucharist is celebrated. The fact that there were no church buildings at this time does not exclude the use of altars in Christian homes or other meeting places.

25 This seems to allude to Jesus's words in Mt 18:19,20 where he speaks of two or three gathered in prayer in his name.

26 A quotation from Prov 3:34 which is also quoted by James (4:6) and Peter (1 Pet 5:5).

27 A bishop is a steward of God's flock. His obligation is faithful pastoral leadership of his church, always remembering that he will answer to God for his stewardship (see Mt 20:1-16). The duty of the faithful is to receive the bishop as God's appointed leader (cf. Lk 10:16, "he who hears you hears me").

28 "Heresy" means a sect that breaks off from the whole. The word later came to have a specific meaning of doctrinal aberration. Heresy is a sin against truth; schism (Greek *schisma*) is a sin against love. No Christian should countenance

midst. Nor do you listen to anyone more than the one who speaks about Jesus Christ in truth.

Chapter 7

(1) For some are accustomed to bear the name [of Christ] with an evil guile while practicing other things that are unworthy of God. These are ones you should avoid like wild beasts for they are mad dogs, biting behind others' backs. These are some whom you must guard yourselves against because they are hard to heal. (2) There is one physician,[29] both fleshly and spiritual, born and unborn,[30] becoming God in the flesh, true life in death, from Mary and from God, at first suffering then incapable of suffering.[31] This is Jesus Christ our Lord.

---

either. God desires his people to walk in truth (*contra heresy*) and in loving unity (*contra schism*).

29 The entirety of section 7:2 is important for the patristic emphasis on Christ as the physician (*iatros*). Even though this title is implied in Jesus's own words in Mt 9:12, Mk 2:17, and Lk 5:31, the NT does not use the word directly of Christ except by his taunters (Lk 4:23). Conceiving of sin and its effects as a disease, the fathers see the church as a hospital for sinners with Christ as the chief physician.

30 *gennetos* and *agennetos* ("born and unborn"). From the parallel statements around it, Ignatius clearly means *gennetos* with respect to Christ's humanity and *aggenetos* with respect to his divinity. This has caused considerable confusion in the history of Christian thought because *gennetos* is used by later writers to mean "begotten" as in the Nicene Creed when it says, "begotten, not made." Later orthodox writers say that the Eternal Son is begotten (*gennetos*) from the Father from eternity and did not become God (*genetos*). In that later usage, *gennetos* (begotten) is used of Christ's divinity whereas Ignatius is clearly using it of Christ's humanity. The historical complications in the distinction between *genetos* and *gennetos* are discussed by J.B. Lighfoot vol. 2 p. 90-94. Suffice it to say that Ignatius is using the terms without the later precision that became necessary in the Arian struggles of the 4th century.

31 By using the temporal phrases "at first" and "then" Ignatius is referring to the death and resurrection of Jesus. The term "incapable of suffering" or "beyond suffering" is *apathes*. It will be used by later writers to signify an eternal attribute

Chapter 8

(1) Let no one deceive you, as you in fact are not deceived, since you are wholly God's. For when no dissension[32] that can torment you has arisen, then you are living by God's will. As scum of the earth[33] I sanctify myself for you Ephesians, for the church famous for ages. (2) Those who are fleshly cannot practice spiritual things nor can those who are spiritual practice fleshly things just as faith cannot do the things of unbelief nor unbelief the things of faith.[34] Even the things you practice according to the flesh are spiritual for you practice them in Jesus Christ.[35]

---

of God called the impassibility of God, i.e. that God does not experience the same ups and downs of emotion that human beings feel. While his writings do not explore this idea, Ignatius may be one of the sources for the later development of the idea by his insistence that Jesus Christ has transferred into the heavenly realm that is beyond the vicissitudes of earthly corruption.

32 Chapter 8 is yet another exhortation to unity and love. Here the Antiochean bishop reveals his Pauline roots by speaking of sanctifying himself for the unity and spiritual welfare of the Ephesian church. His own devotion to spiritual things, he hopes, will inspire them to see the difference between a sinful (fleshy) way of life and following the Spirit of God. For those who are of faith and the Spirit, even their normal lives in the world are spiritual because they are "in Jesus Christ."

33 Ignatius uses *peripsema*, translated by Holmes as "humble sacrifice." Ehrman translates this as "I give myself as a sacrificial offering." LS gives the meaning of "anything wiped off, i.e. of a vile person or scapegoat." Ignatius speaks in self-deprecating terms as he gives his life as a self-offering. By the world he is regarded as a criminal but in God's plan of salvation (*oikonomia*) his sufferings benefit the church.

34 Ignatius's vocabulary in 8.2 is clearly drawn from Paul's stark contrast between the flesh and the Spirit. The closest parallel to this text is probably 1 Cor 2:13,14. In Paul and in Ignatius there is an intentional ambiguity in the phrase "according to the flesh" (*kata sarka*). Here and in Paul's Romans 1:3 it refers to "human nature" or "things done in everyday life" without any connotations of sin, whereas in Romans 8:13 *kata sarka* connotes a sinful way of life as Ignatius's "fleshly things" (*ta sarkika*) does here.

35 "In Jesus Christ" is modeled on the Pauline doctrine of being "in Christ." Paul's doctrine of the incorporation of the faithful into Christ pervades his letters.

Chapter 9

(1) I recognized some who were passing through there with evil doctrine. You have not permitted them to sow [evil doctrine] among you, because you have plugged up your ears as not to receive the things sown by them. As stones of the Father's temple you have been prepared to be God the Father's building, lifted up to the heights through the crane[36] of Jesus Christ, which is the cross, as you use the Holy Spirit for a rope. Your faith is your guide;[37] love is the way that carries you up to God. (2) You are all fellow travelers,[38] God-bearers, temple-bearers, Christ-bearers, bearers of holiness, ordered well in every way in the commands of Jesus Christ. For you I was joyfully made worthy to communicate with you in writing and to rejoice with you that you love no other life than God.[39]

Chapter 10

(1) Pray unceasingly for others; in their case there is hope for repentance, that they may obtain God. Permit them to become disciples by [seeing] your works. (2) With regard to their expres-

---

Baptism is the initial and definitive act of this incorporation of believers into Christ (see Paul Rom 6:1-5). Through the giving of the Spirit in baptism, the baptized become members of the body of Christ (see 1 Cor 12:13).

36 "crane" is a traditional translation of *machane*, a word that means any kind of implement or instrument (cf. Italian *machina*, English *machine*).

37 "guide" here is *anagogeus*, a guide that leads upward. It can refer to people, to physical objects (e.g. straps) or, as here, to abstract things like faith.

38 "fellow travelers" is *synodos*. It is not a common word in Greek literature and can mean a "joint assembly" as well.

39 Ignatius here expresses an idea always emphasized in the later spiritual writers of the church, especially those in the eastern monastic traditions. The sacraments and all the other temporal aids to the spiritual life are designed to foster a love for God alone who is the ultimate final goal of Christian living.

sions of anger, be meek; with regard to their boasts, be humble. Meet their blasphemies with your prayers and their deception with your steadfastness of faith. Meet their unruly life with your gentleness, and be diligent not to imitate them. (3) Let us be found to be their brothers in gentleness and diligent to be imitators of the Lord. Who has been more wronged? Who has been defrauded? Who has been rejected?[40] This is so that no weed[41] of the devil may be found among you but that in purity and sobriety you may remain in Jesus Christ both bodily and spiritually.

Chapter 11

(1) These are the last times. So finally, let us shrink back;[42] let us fear the patience of God that it may not become judgment for us. For we should either fear the coming wrath or love the present grace.[43] One or the other. Only being found in Christ Jesus leads to true life. (2) Apart from him nothing is appropriate. In him I carry around these bonds, my spiritual pearls.[44] In these may it be granted to me to rise again through your prayers. May I always be a partaker [of this resurrection] so that I may be

---

40 With Ehrman, I take the implied subject of these questions to be Jesus Christ, i.e. "who has been more mistreated than he?" Holmes interprets it differently.

41 Ignatius uses the botanical metaphor only to refer to demonic influence (cf. Trall 6:1). *Botane* can be "planting, plant, or weed."

42 Holmes takes *aischunthomen* as "let us be reverent" whereas Ehrman translates it as "so we should feel ashamed." In the NT, it is normally translated "be ashamed." Ignatius seems to be using it in the same negative sense as 1 Jn 2:28, "Let us not shrink back from him at his coming." Ignatius is urging an attitude of reverence and holy fear in the face of who God is.

43 "the present grace" is God's forbearance in not bringing judgment on the world. It is by loving the grace of God that we avoid the future judgment because in Christ both the present and future are under divine mercy.

44 Later Christian writers speak of the bonds of imprisonment or martyrdom as pearls. See Lightfoot vol. 2 p. 62.

found in the company of the Ephesian Christians who always agree with[45] the apostles in the power of Jesus Christ.

Chapter 12

(1) I know who I am, and to whom I write. I am condemned, but you have received mercy. I am in danger; you are secure. (2) You are the way for those who are being slaughtered for God;[46] you are fellow initiates with Paul [into the mysteries].[47] This Paul was sanctified, he was confirmed by the testimony,[48] and he is worthy of the greatest blessing. May I also be found to walk in his footsteps whenever I reach God. In every letter Paul mentions you in Christ Jesus.

Chapter 13

(1) So, be diligent to gather more frequently[49] for thanksgiving and glory to God.[50] For whenever you gather in the

---

45 Some MSS have *suniemi* (understand) and others have *suaineo* (agree with).

46 *anaireo* ("slaughtered") can also mean "take up" and so the translation would be "taken up to God." Perhaps Ignatius intentionally chose an ambigious word to show that by his being slain for God, he will find this path to God through the service that the Ephesians render to him.

47 *summustai* ("fellow initiates"). This word implies being initiated into the mysteries. This word and many cognates will be used by later Christian writers to refer to the sacraments of initiation (Baptism, Chrismation, Eucharist). In this context, Ignatius again draws on the Pauline teaching of the real communication of spiritual goods in the body of Christ. Not only does Ephesus lie on the road to Rome, the Ephesian Christians are the means for his attaining martyrdom and thus God in his death. See Camelot p. 68.

48 *memartuemenou* ("confirmed by the testimony") means that his witness for Christ with his life secured his place in heaven.

49 Most take *puknos* temporally as "more frequently" but it may have a spatial reference meaning "more closely together," i.e. in closer union with one another.

50 *eucharistia* ("for thanksgiving and glory to God") as used here may simply be "thanksgiving" or it may also refer to the eucharistic liturgy. Ignatius already uses the term as a designation of the church's worship. See Philad 4:1; Smyrn 7:1; 8:1.

same place frequently, the powers of Satan are annihilated, and his destructive intention is destroyed in your harmony of faith. (2) Nothing is better than peace. In it, every war in heaven and on earth is brought to nothing.[51]

Chapter 14

(1) Nothing escapes your notice if you have faith and love[52] completely in Jesus Christ. This is the beginning and the end of life. Faith is the beginning; love is the end.[53] When the two are in harmony, God is there. Everything else leading to a noble character follows from this.[54] (2) No one claiming faith lives in sin, nor does one possessing love persist in hate.[55] "The tree is known from its fruits;"[56] thus, those who claim to belong to Christ will be evident from the things they do. For the work is not a matter of what one claims now, but it is a matter of being found in the power of faith at the end.

---

51 Chapter 13 shows the true character of the liturgy as an engagement with cosmic powers, a theme that will show up in the homilies of St. John Chrysostom in the late fourth century. This explains why unity and harmony in the church, especially as found in the liturgy, is so important. The church on earth is like an army engaging in warfare against the forces of darkness when it worships the true God in unity and love under the proper authority of a bishop.

52 Ignatius, like Paul in 1 Cor 13, speaks of faith and love as twin virtues. Real faith naturally leads to love and is completed by love.

53 Cf. 1 Cor 13:8, "Love never fails," and 13:13, "Now these three remain: faith, hope, and love, but the greatest of these is love."

54 Ignatius here conceives of unity both as unity among the members of the church and unity within the heart of individuals. True unity has both an objective and a subjective aspect.

55 Ignatius sounds much like the apostle John in 1 Jn 3:6, "Everyone who abides in him does not sin." For both Ignatius and John the worst manifestation of sin is hate. See 1 Jn 3:15, "Everyone who hates is a murderer, and you know that no murderer has eternal life remaining in him."

56 See Mt 12:33.

Chapter 15

(1) It is better to keep silent and to truly be, than to speak and not be. To teach is good if the one speaking acts [in accord with his teaching]. Therefore, there is one Teacher, who spoke and it happened. And the things he did in silence are worthy of the Father.[57] (2) The one who possesses Jesus's word can truly also hear his silence, that he may be perfect, that he may act through what he says and be known by his silence.[58] Nothing escapes the Lord's notice, but even our hidden affairs are known to him. (3) Let us do everything as if it comes from him who is dwelling[59] in us, that we may be his temples and that our God may be in us, which in fact he is. This will become apparent to us when we rightly love him.[60]

Chapter 16

(1) Do not be deceived, my brothers; those who corrupt homes will not inherit the kingdom of God. (2) So if those who are doing these things according to the flesh die, how much more, if they corrupt the faith of God[61] in evil teaching? Jesus

---

57 Does this refer to the hidden years of Jesus's life? On the silence of God in Ignatius see also the comments at Eph 19:1.

58 The value that Ignatius places on silence will become a major theme in Eastern spirituality. The heyschast movement (Greek *hesuchia* = silence) becomes strong in the fourth century and provokes controversy in the age of Gregory Palamas (14th century).

59 The phrase, "as if it comes from him who is dwelling," may mean "as if it belongs to him who dwells in us." Ehrman and Camelot insert the verb "know," i.e. "knowing that he is dwelling in us." I see no reason to assume that Ignatius means anything other than the way I have translated it.

60 Here Ignatius draws on Paul's doctrine of the church and its individual members as temples of God as in 1 Cor 3:16, 6:19, and 2 Cor 6:16. This language would have been familiar to the Ephesian Christians through Paul's letter to them. See Paul Eph 2:20-22.

61 *pistin theou* ("faith of God") probably means "the faith established by God" or

Christ was crucified for this [faith]. Such a man, because he is defiled, will end up in unquenchable fire. The same is true for the one who listens to him.[62]

Chapter 17

(1) For this reason the Lord received ointment on his head to breathe incorruptibility[63] on the church. Do not be anointed with the foul smell of this world's ruler's teaching,[64] lest he keep you as a prisoner from living the life set before you. (2) Why do we not all become wise when we receive the knowledge of God, which is Jesus Christ? Why do we foolishly die, by ignoring the gift which the Lord truly sent?

Chapter 18

(1) My spirit is in sacrificial service for the cross,[65] which is a scandal to unbelievers, but to us it is salvation and eternal life. Where are the wise? Where is the debater? Where is the

---

what theologians call the *fides quae creditur*. This is the meaning in Jude 3 of "the faith once handed down to the saints" (i.e. God's holy people). It is the same meaning as in "the Christian Faith," i.e. the objective content of the faith rather than the subjective faith of a person.

62 Ignatius sounds a note familiar to ancient Christians but often opprobrious to modern ones. Heresy that is embraced knowledgeably and consciously involves a rejection of divinely revealed truth and imperils eternal salvation.

63 See Mt 26:6-13. See also John 20:19-23 about Jesus breathing on the Apostles. Ignatius here begins the patristic practice of drawing out spiritual applications for the church from the specific historical events of Christ's life. See Eph 18:2 about baptism. Meditating on the events of Christ's life is a way of entering into the mysteries of salvation. Ignatius of Loyola founded his *Spiritual Exercises* on this practice.

64 See Paul 2 Cor 2:15, "we are the aroma of Christ to God" and Eph 5:2.

65 "Sacrificial service" is *peripsema* which carries two ideas: sacrifice and self-abasement. See note at Eph 8:1.

boast of those called intelligent?[66] (2) Our God, Jesus the Christ, was conceived by Mary according to God's design;[67] he is from the seed of David and of the Holy Spirit. He was born and baptized that he might purify the water by his Passion.[68]

Chapter 19

(1) Mary's virginity and giving birth escaped the notice of the ruler of this age,[69] as did the death of the Lord. There are three mysteries[70] that cry out; these were done in the silence of God.[71] (2) So how was it shown to the ages? A star in heaven

---

66 These questions draw on 1 Cor 1:20-23.

67 *oikonomia* ("design") is a word used by Paul and many later church fathers, especially Irenaeus. It denotes the plan of salvation or God's design for the redemption of the human race.

68 The NT letters do not comment much on the events of Christ's life. The early church fathers began commenting on specific events such as the birth and the baptism. For an exception see 2 Pet 1:17,18 where Peter mentions the Transfiguration. Later fathers will interpret Jesus's baptism in the Jordan as an act of cleansing all waters for the baptism of sinners. This draws on Paul's doctrine of baptism as union with the passion of Christ in Rom 6:1ff.

69 See 1 Cor 2:7,8, "But we speak God's wisdom hidden in a mystery which God established before the ages for our glory. None of the rulers of this age have known this wisdom for had they known it, they would not have crucified the Lord of glory." Ignatius uses the singular "ruler" (*archonta*), referring clearly to the Evil One, while Paul uses the plural (*archonton*) and may be referring to human rulers. Ignatius may be drawing on John's language as much as Paul's. See "the ruler of this world" (*kosmos*) in Jn 16:11.

70 The Greek word *musterion* has a rich meaning in Christian usage, starting in the NT. Paul, for example, uses *musterion* to refer to God's plan (*oikonomia*) in Eph 3:1-7. See v. 4, "in the mystery of Christ" (cf. Col 1:26). Here Ignatius initiates a long tradition of referring to the events of the life of Christ and of redemptive history in general as "mysteries." Later Christian writers will use the plural *mysteria* to refer to the sacraments.

71 *hesuchia* ("silence"). See Eph 15:2, "He who possesses Jesus's word can also hear his silence." There Ignatius is encouraging silence in those who teach; here he

shone more brightly than all the stars, and its radiance was inexpressible, and its novelty produced wonder. All the other stars,
along with the sun and the moon, formed a chorus for that star.
The radiance of that star far exceeded any other, and the source
of this incomparable novelty caused a disturbance. (3) Therefore
every [form of magic] and every bondage has been destroyed;
ignorance that comes from evil[72] has vanished; the old kingdom
is destroyed. It is corrupted in a human sense when God appears
for the renewal of eternal life. That which has been prepared
receives its foundation with God. Therefore all things are stirred
up because the destruction of death is taken care of.

Chapter 20

(1) If Jesus Christ counts me worthy by your prayer, and it
is his will, in a second treatise that I am about to write, I will
show you the plan which I began leading to the new man, Jesus
Christ in his faith, and in his love, in his suffering, and resurrection.[73] (2) This is especially the case if the Lord shows me
that each of you gathers together in one faith and in one
Jesus Christ who came from the stock of David in the flesh,
the Son of Man and Son of God. This results in you obeying
your bishop and your presbytery with undistracted mind as

---

refers to the eternal plan in which redemption was foreordained. We see Paul in
Rom 16:25, "according to the revelation of the mystery that has been held in
silence for long ages." See also Paul Eph 3:9.

72 There are different punctuations in this text resulting in different translations.
I have followed Holmes who takes "evil" as modifying "ignorance" while Ehrman
takes "evil" in conjunction with "bondage." Both are possible.

73 I have translated these prepositional phrases literally to allow the reader to
interpret them. "In his faith" probably means "in faith in him" and "in his love"
probably means "in love for him." So Holmes and Camelot translate; Ehrman
renders it "involving his faithfulness and love."

you break bread[74] which is the medicine of immortality,[75] the antidote against death and life forever through Jesus Christ.

Chapter 21

(1) I am your substitute soul,[76] and for those that you sent to Smyrna for the honor of God. So I write to you, giving thanks to the Lord, and giving my love to Polycarp as well as to you. Remember me as Jesus Christ also remembers you. (2) Pray for the church that is in Syria. I am going to Rome in chains. I, the least of all believers there, was counted worthy to be found for the honor of God. Farewell in God the Father and in Jesus Christ, our common hope.

---

74 "Breaking bread" is the expression used by Luke in Acts for the eucharistic celebration. See Acts 2:46; 20:7,11. In the NT period, "breaking bread" may have also meant a larger meal of which the Eucharist was a part.

75 On this important phrase in Ignatius, see chapter five in the introductory essays.

76 *antipsuchon* ("substitute soul") occurs four times in the letters (see also Smyrn 10:2; Polyc 2:3; 6:1). It is difficult to translate. Ehrman has "I am giving my life for you" while Holmes has the weaker "I am devoted to you." Camelot uses "ransom" and explains that it carries the idea of one life in exchange for another. The word does not occur in the NT but the concept is expressed in Jn 15:13 and in the ransom (*lutron*) of Mk 10:45.

Chapter Eight
Ignatius's Letter to the Magnesians
Translation and Commentary

The *Letter to the Magnesians* emphasizes the theme of obedience to the rightful bishop. Damas (see 2:1) was probably a younger man (see 3:1,2) who was fighting the docetic heresy troubling the churches of Asia Minor. Ancient Magnesia lay on the Maiander river but was not an especially important city. We do not know how Christianity first arrived there. The contents of the letter clearly presuppose an alternative church, or at least liturgy (see 4:1), as seems to be the case in other cities. This opposing assembly must have had some Jews who were claiming that being a disciple of Jesus did not preclude — or possibly required — following Jewish laws and customs, a problem evident in the NT itself (cf. Acts 15; Galatians). As in the other letters, Ignatius here emphasizes the unity of the church in both outward and inward aspects.

Salutation

Ignatius, called Theophorus, to the [church] blessed in the grace of God the Father in Christ Jesus our Savior. In him I greet the church that is in Magnesia on the Maiander and I ask for great greetings in God the Father and in Jesus Christ.

Chapter 1

(1) Since I recognized with joy the well-ordered nature of your love in God, I chose ahead of time to speak to you in the faith of Jesus Christ. (2) By being made worthy of the God-fitting name, as I carry these bonds, I sing the praises of the churches in which I beg for the unity of the flesh and the spirit of Jesus Christ,[1] our constant life; and I beg for the unity of faith and love. Nothing is to be preferred to this. Even more important is that union of Jesus and the Father.[2] If in him we endure every insult of the ruler of this age and take refuge in God, we shall obtain it.[3]

---

1   "unity of the flesh and spirit of Jesus Christ" may refer to the human and divine natures of Christ or to his humanity (flesh) and the Holy Spirit who filled Jesus in his earthly ministry. In this context, Ignatius asks that the same unity which characterized Jesus's own union of the divine and human within himself would fill members of the church.

2   "that union of Jesus and the Father" could also be translated "that union with Jesus and the Father." Both meanings have important implications for Ignatius's theology. He teaches that Jesus is perfectly united to the Father and that this same union should be manifested in the church.

3   It is not clear what Ignatius is saying we will obtain. The context suggests that the union of flesh and spirit, as well as of faith and love, will come through enduring all the insults and sufferings that the Devil can throw at the church. The Enemy of the church intends to tear it apart but endurance in these trials means remaining as one.

Chapter 2

(1) Since I was counted worthy to see you through Damas your God-worthy bishop and your worthy presbyters Bassus, and Apollonius, as well as through my fellow servant, the deacon Zotion, I have benefited from him because he is subject to the bishop as to the grace of God and to the presbytery as to the law of Jesus Christ.

Chapter 3

(1) And it is fitting for you not to abuse[4] the age of your bishop, but that you show all respect according to the power of God the Father, as I also knew the holy presbyters have not abused the present order which appears to be more youthful,[5] but as those who are wisely docile to him in God. Yet they are docile not to him, but to the Father of Jesus Christ, the bishop of all. (2) So it is fitting to obey without any hypocrisy for the honor of that One who willed this since [in disobedience] a person is deceiving not the bishop who can be seen, but is attempting to defraud the Invisible Bishop.[6] The matter is not just a human affair, but has to do with God who knows the hidden things.[7]

---

4 *sugchrasthai* ("abuse") is translated by Holmes and Ehrman as "take advantage of." The word is used in both positive and negative senses. Ignatius here commands that no one use the bishop's age as an excuse for irreverence or disobedience.

5 "the present order which appears to be more youthful." This is a fairly literal translation but it seems to mean that the present bishop is being respected by the presbyters in spite of his youthful appearance.

6 Ignatius calls God a bishop because he knows that *episkopos* means "overseer" and that the cognate verb *episkopeo* means "oversee."

7 Ignatius stresses that the church hierarchy is divinely sanctioned and therefore obedience to the bishop is not a matter of outward show but of inward assent. He implies that judgment will come on the person who lives only in superficial

Chapter 4

(1) It is appropriate not only to be called a Christian but in fact to be one. This would be like those who use the title "bishop" but do everything apart from him. Such ones do not appear to me to have a good conscience because they certainly do not hold their assemblies in accord with the commandment.[8]

Chapter 5

(1) These matters have a purpose[9] and two things lie before us together.[10] One is death and the other is life. Each one will end up in its own place. (2) As there are two types of coins,[11] one of God and the other of the world and each of them has a distinctive stamp[12] on them, [so] unbelievers have that of the world, and believers have the stamp of God the Father in love through Jesus Christ. If we do not willingly

---

obedience to the bishop without a heartfelt consent. The last sentence about God knowing the hidden things reiterates a common scriptural theme found in Col 3:22, "Slaves, obey your human masters in every way, not in outward service but in simplicity of heart with reverence for the Lord." On God judging the hidden things, see Paul Rom 2:16 and 1 Cor 4:5.

8   *kata entolen* ("in accord with the commandment") means presumably the command of the bishop or the Christian rule of doing everything under the guidance of the bishop.

9   "purpose" is *telos* = goal, aim. The reason for the authority of bishops, presbyters, and deacons in the church is to lead the faithful to life. This chapter reflects the contrast between the two ways described in the *Didache,* chapters 1,2. See also Mt 7:13,14.

10 See the Holmes and Ehrman translations.

11 *nomismata* ("coins") literally means "currencies." A coin bears an imprint in the same way that the Christian bears the imprint of God. This is part of the foundation for the idea that baptism places an indelible mark on the soul. See chapter four in the introductory essays for a discussion of *character.*

12 Our word "character" is a transliteration of the word used here meaning a "stamp" or an "imprint." The word is used of Jesus as the exact imprint of the essence of the Father in Heb 1:3.

embrace dying for his passion, neither is his life in us.[13]

Chapter 6

(1) So, since I have seen the entire congregation in the aforementioned persons, I exhort you to be diligent to practice everything in harmony with God, as the bishop leads in the place of God and the presbyters in the place of the council of the apostles and of the deacons — those sweetest to me — who have been entrusted with the service[14] of Jesus Christ who was with the Father before all ages and has appeared at the end [of the world].[15] (2) By receiving a character like God's, honor one another and let no one view his neighbor according to human standards.[16] Rather, love one another in Jesus Christ always. Let there be nothing among you that can divide you but be united to the bishop and to those presiding for the imprint and teaching of incorruptibility.[17]

---

13 Here Ignatius draws on the Pauline theme of dying and rising with Christ as expressed in Rom 6:1ff and Phil 3:8-12.

14 *diakonia* generally means "service" but came to designate the work of deacons as tending to the physical and material needs of others. It is used in the NT in both senses.

15 Christ appeared at the end of the ages. See Rom 16:25,26. In Gal 4:4, Paul says "when the fullness of time came, God sent forth his son ..."

16 "according to human standards," *kata sarka* means literally "according to the flesh." Ignatius seems to mean the phrase in the sense that Paul uses it in 2 Cor 5:16, "If we have known Christ *kata sarka*, we know him this way no longer."

17 Camelot has an insightful comment: "For Ignatius, as for the New Testament and the Greek fathers of the church, this incorruptibility is immortality, eternal life, an essentially divine attribute in which man cannot participate except through the gift of God," p. 99.

Chapter 7

(1) As the Lord [Jesus] did nothing without the Father because he was united to him — whether he did it by himself or through the apostles — neither should you practice anything without the bishop or the presbyters. Neither should you try anything that appears to be fine on your own but you should always do the same thing: one prayer, one petition, one mind, one hope in love, in a spotless joy — this is Jesus Christ than whom nothing is better. (2) All of you should come together to one temple of God, as on one altar, to one Jesus Christ who came forth from the one Father, was one being, and will return.

Chapter 8

(1) Do not be deceived by heterodox teachings or old myths that are unprofitable. If we have lived till now by the law,[18] we confess that we have received grace. (2) The most divine prophets lived in accord with Christ Jesus. For this reason, they were persecuted while being inspired by this grace so that the disobedient might be convinced that there is one God who made himself known through Jesus Christ his Son. He is the Word proceeding from silence and who in every way pleased the one who sent him.[19]

---

18 Some MSS have "Judaism" instead of "law."

19 The Word coming forth from silence has provoked much discussion among scholars. There was probably a corruption of the text that entered very early in the transmission process. Most scholars accept the text as literally translated above (*logos apo siges proelthon*). The "silence" referred to was a major theme of Gnosticism in the later second century but Ignatius's words could reflect an earlier form of the heresy floating around Asia Minor. He is probably thinking here of the Incarnation — God becoming man — rather than the eternal generation of the Son within the Trinity.

Chapter 9

(1) If those who lived in the old ways come to the newness of hope, they no longer keep the Sabbath but live by the Lord's Day. On this day, our life dawned through him and his death, which some deny. Through this mystery we have received faith[20] and for this reason we endure that we may be found to be disciples of Jesus Christ, our only teacher. (2) How can we live without him whom the prophets, since they were his disciples by the Spirit, were expecting as their teacher? For this reason the one for whom they rightly waited raised them from the dead when he arrived.[21]

Chapter 10

Let us be not unaware of his goodness. If he imitated our practices, we would no longer exist. Therefore, when we become his disciples, let us learn to live according to Christianity.[22] Whoever is called by another name than this one is not of God. (2) Put away the evil leaven, that has grown old and sour, and be changed[23] into new leaven which is Jesus Christ. Be salted in him

---

20 *to pisteuein* ("faith") is an infinitive and so emphasizes the act of believing. For Ignatius, faith is a gift contained in the Paschal Mystery. Every Lord's Day (Sunday) recalls and mystically reenacts Christ's death and resurrection. In the liturgy the gift of faith is available to all who will take hold of it.

21 Is this last sentence about being raised from the dead an allusion to Mt 27:52,53?

22 Ignatius is the first writer to use the term "Christianity." No doubt it was modeled on the existing word "Judaism." Here we see the beginnings of the widening gulf between Judaism and Christianity. Perhaps it is not an accident that it should arise from Antioch since it was there that the disciples was first called Christians (Acts 11:26). Ignatius uses the term also in Philad 6:1 and "Christian" in Rom 3:1.

23 *metabalesthe* ("be changed"). There are different ways the verb may be translated. One is "reach for" (Holmes) or "turn to" (Ehrman). Bauer uses *zuwenden* ("turn to") while Camelot has *transformez-vous* ("transform yourself"). The Protestant

that no one may be corrupted since you will be repelled[24] by the odor. (3) It is out of place to speak of Jesus Christ and practice Judaism. Christianity was not entrusted[25] to Judaism but Judaism to Christianity. Every tongue that believes this was gathered to God.[26]

Chapter 11

(1) My beloved, [I write] these things not because I knew some of you to be like this but, as one who is more insignificant, I want to protect you that you not fall into the trap[27] of empty glory[28] but that you fully participate[29] in the birth, passion, and resurrection that happened in the time of the governor Pontius Pilate. These things were really and truly done by Jesus Christ, our hope, from which not one of you should turn aside.[30]

---

scholars, reading it as middle voice, tend not to see any deeper significance in the word while Camelot, probably reading it as a passive, may have been aware of the use of *metaballo* in the later fathers where the word is used, among other applications, for the transformation of the bread and wine into the body and blood of Christ.

24 *elegchthesesthe* ("repelled"), lit. "be rebuked." Ehrmann translates, "show for what you are" and Camelot, "you will be judged."

25 *Episteusan* ("entrusted"). Most translators use "Christianity did not believe in Judaism, etc." "Believed" is used in the sense that Judaism had its goal and fulfillment in Christianity. Thus "entrusted" means that the economy of salvation in the old covenant finds its fulfillment in the new.

26 See Is 66:18.

27 "trap" is literally *angiston*, "(fish) hook."

28 For "empty glory" Ehrman has "worthless ideas" but this flattens the full meaning of *kenodoxia*. The older English "vainglory" is closer to the Greek.

29 *peplerophoresthai* ("fully participate"). This sometimes means "fully convinced or confident." Ignatius probably means that the Magnesians would find the fullness of their life in the events of Christ's Paschal Mystery. This is consistent with the exhortations of chapter 10.

30 The emphasis on the historical reality of Jesus's life has a double importance. It countered the docetic tendencies which said that Jesus only appeared to be a

Chapter 12

(1) May I benefit from you in every way if indeed I am worthy. For since I am bound [in chains] I am not like even one of you who are at liberty. I know that you are not puffed up. You have Jesus Christ in you. Rather, when I praise you, I know you are reverent,[31] as is written because "the righteous is his own accuser."[32]

Chapter 13

So be diligent to be confirmed in the teachings of the Lord and of the apostles that whatever you do, you be prospered[33] in flesh and spirit, in faith and love, in the Son and the Father and the Spirit, in the beginning and at the end.[34] This all is with your worthy bishop and presbytery that is worthy of the woven crown and the godly deacons. (2) Be subject to your bishop and to one another, as Jesus Christ in the flesh is to the Father and the apostles to Christ, the Father, and the Spirit. The result is that your unity will be both physical and spiritual.[35]

---

man and it called Christians to internalize the events of Christ's life for their own salvation.

31 *entrepesthe* ("reverent"). This verb can also mean "be ashamed" and is so translated by Holmes, Bauer, and Camelot. I have chosen "reverent" because Ignatius seems to say something positive about the Magnesians.

32 See Prov 18:17.

33 "whatever you do, you be prospered." This is almost an exact quotation from Ps 1:3 in the LXX. *Kateuodothete* means more lit. "be led well along the way."

34 All these couplets ("in flesh and spirit, in faith and love, in the Son and the Father and the Spirit, in the beginning and at the end") are the ways in which the Christian prospers, not in a worldly sense, but in the work of God. Spiritual well-being is tied up with being confirmed and strengthened in the teachings of the Lord and his apostles.

35 Here Ignatius expresses the two sides of the church, the outward and the inward. Unity must be both. It is not enough to profess unity in spirit without a

Chapter 14

Because I know that you are filled with God, I commanded you briefly. Remember me in your prayers that I may attain to God and to the church in Syria from which I am not worthy to be called.[36] I appeal to the unity of your prayer and love in God that the church in Syria may be worthy to be bedewed[37] through your churches.

Chapter 15

The Ephesians greet you from Smyrna[38] from where I write as they are ready for the glory of God just as you are. They have refreshed me in every way together with Polycarp, the bishop of the Smyrneans. And the rest of the churches greet you in the honor of Jesus Christ.

---

tangible expression of that unity in the visible church. The modern notion of a purely "spiritual" union without the hierarchical structure is something that Ignatius and the whole catholic tradition utterly rejects.

36 Holmes, Camelot, and Bauer insert the word "member," i.e. Ignatius is not worthy to be called a member of the church in Syria. They also take the phrase "the church in Syria" to be the object of "remember" and so Ignatius is asking for remembrance in prayer for himself and for the church in Syria. Ignatius could also be implying that he is not worthy to be the bishop of the church in Syria and also that he wishes to attain to God and to the level of holiness exhibited by the members of the Syrian church. It would not be the last time in history when a priest expressed his conviction that the members of his flock exceeded him in holiness.

37 Chapter 14 expresses the idea of participatory sharing among the members of the church. The prayers of the church in Magnesia will result in an outpouring of the Holy Spirit implied in the words "be bedewed." Prayer united to God in love will cause God's grace to be poured out upon other members of the body of Christ.

38 Here is an indication that Ignatius had already been in Ephesus and is writing from Smyrna.

Chapter Nine
Ignatius's Letter to the Trallians
Translation and Commentary

The *Letter to the Trallians* appears to have been written from
Smyrna after Ignatius had visited Ephesus as indicated in Trall
12:1. Obedience to the rightful authority of the bishop appears
here, as it does in all the other letters, to be grounded in divine
authority (2:1). Ignatius commends the Trallians for their love
for Polybius their bishop (1:1). He refers to the sacraments as
"mysteries" (2:3) and specifically the Eucharist as renewing faith
and love in the faithful (8:1). Ignatius is countering some form
of Docetism with this letter. He roundly condemns the Docetists'
pride in heavenly visions (cf. 5:2), in mixing Christ with their
own ideas (6:2), in their rejection of the altar of the church
(7:2), and, most of all, in their denial of the real humanity of
Jesus Christ (9:1). Ignatius urges the Trallians that the best
weapon against heresy and schism is meekness (3:2), love
(13:2), and deep union with Christ in his passion (11:2).

Salutation

Ignatius, called Theophorus, to the holy church of Tralles in Asia, beloved by God, the Father of Jesus Christ. This church is chosen and worthy of God, living in peace in both flesh and spirit[1] by the passion of Jesus Christ,[2] our hope. You live in the resurrection leading to him.[3] I greet you in the fullness,[4] in apostolic authority,[5] and I wish you the warmest greetings.

---

1 "in flesh and spirit." Ignatius uses the phrase in several letters to refer to the external and the internal. The church is "beloved, chosen, and worthy of God" in both its outward governance and in its inner peace.

2 "by the passion of Jesus Christ." Ignatius speaks often of the passion (sufferings) of Christ (see e.g. Eph 18:2; 20:1; Mag 11:1; Trall 11:2). Here the dative case may be expressing the means ("by") or the idea of "with respect to." In either case, Ignatius affirms that the peace and welfare of the church flows from union with the sufferings and resurrection of Christ.

3 "in the resurrection leading to him." My translation is somewhat loose but it does express two important ideas. The current earthly life of the church flows from the resurrection of Jesus and the final resurrection on the last day has as its goal complete union with Jesus Christ ("to him").

4 Does this mean the fullness of grace and of the Spirit of Christ, as Camelot takes it, or "out of a full heart" (*aus vollem Herzen*) as Bauer takes it? Or could it be in the fullness of authority? An argument for this last reading would derive from seeing the following phrase *en apostoloko characteri* as an apposition to fullness. See the next note.

5 *en apostoloko characteri* ("in apostolic authority"). The word *character* in Greek means a stamp or impression of one thing on something else. Ignatius uses it in Mag 5:2 (see comment there). Most Protestants (e.g. Bauer, Holmes) translate this "in an apostolic manner." This is probably too weak since *character* has a more forceful meaning than *tropos* ("manner") or some such synonym. Bauer points to 3:3 and Rom 4:3 as evidence that Ignatius cannot be claiming apostolic authority. Those texts show Ignatius's awareness that he is not an apostle but this does not exclude his having a derived apostolic authority just as calling himself a deacon does not mean he was not a bishop. His authority carries the full weight of the truth of the gospel inherited from the apostles. This expression may be a way of speaking of this apostolic succession. See chapter 4 on the church in the introductory essays.

Chapter 1

(1) I knew that you possessed a blameless and non-judgmental attitude[6] in endurance. This was not by use but by nature,[7] as Polybius your bishop showed me. He came to Smyrna by the will of God and of Jesus Christ and he rejoiced with me who is bound in Christ Jesus. In him I beheld your entire congregation. (2) Since I received God's good will through him, I glorified God[8] because I found you to be imitators of God, as I knew I would.

Chapter 2

(1) When you are submissive to the bishop as to Jesus Christ, you seem to me to be living not in accord with human custom but in accord with Jesus Christ who died for us. This was so that by believing in his death you may escape dying. (2) As is already your practice, it is necessary to do nothing without [the approval] of the bishop, but to be submissive to the presbytery as to the apostles of Jesus Christ, our hope. We will be found in

---

6 *dianoian adiakriton* ("non-judgmental attitude"). This could be translated several ways. Most translate *adiakriton* as "unwavering" or "steadfast," i.e. in endurance. It could also mean "without distinction" or even "uncritical."

7 "not by use but by nature." The contrast here may reflect one used by the Gnostics in which the majority of church members (the so-called "psychics") possessed virtue "by use" while the elite of the church had virtue "by nature." Ignatius is complimenting the church in Tralles as possessing this blameless mind as an essential part of their life together. Salvation and the acquisition of virtue intimately imply one another. Growth in virtue results in coming closer to God and therefore to salvation.

8 While most translators render this sentence as I have, the word "glorified" could also be translated "honored [Polybius]." It is not clear who the object of the verb (*edoxasa*) is. God? Polybius?

him if we spend our lives for him.[9] (3) The deacons also must be pleasing to all in every way since they are servants of the mysteries of Jesus Christ. For they are not servants of food and drink but helpers of God's church. It is necessary for them to avoid accusations like fire.

Chapter 3

(1) Likewise, all should revere the deacons as Jesus Christ in the same way that the bishop is the exemplar[10] of the Father, and the presbyters are like the council of God and like the bond of the apostles. Apart from these a church cannot be called a church. (2) I am persuaded that this is true of you. I received the token of your love and I have it with me in your bishop whose very bearing is a great instruction. His meekness is [his] power. I think of him just as those who are without God revere him. Because of love I will spare you even though I am able to write more pointedly about this.[11] I did not think that since I am condemned I could command you like an apostle.[12]

---

9   "if we spend our lives for him." The Greek verb *diago* means "to spend time," but the context makes it necessary to infer my translation.

10 *tupos* ("exemplar"). Camelot and Ehrman translate this word as "image." The next verse uses *exemplarion* ("token") which seems interchangeable with *tupos*. *Exemplarion* is also used in Eph 2:1. There Crocus is the token (sign) of love as Polybius is in this text. This expresses the idea of a Christian embodying the love of others as Christ embodied the love of the Father, an idea that assumes the reality of sharing graces in the mystical body of Christ.

11 "about this." This phrase could be translated "in his behalf," i.e. to defend Polybius.

12 All scholars acknowledge that the text of this verse is corrupt. My translation follows a widely accepted pattern. On the implications of not commanding like an apostle, see the note on "apostolic authority" in the salutation of this letter and the introductory essay on the church (chapter 4).

Chapter 4

(1) I have great thoughts in God, but I measure myself [moderately] that I may not die in self-boasting. For now I must fear more than pay attention to those who puff me up. (2) For those who tell me such things are really flogging me because I love suffering but I don't know if I am worthy [of it]. For envy[13] does not appear to [trouble] many but it wages a battle against me. So I use meekness with which the ruler of this age is destroyed.[14]

Chapter 5

(1) Am I not able to write to you of heavenly things? I am afraid lest I do you harm who are [still] babes. Grant me this lest by not being able to contain [these things] you are strangled. (2) And I, though I am bound, I can fix my mind on heavenly things, on the angelic regions, and the ruling guardianship, on things visible and invisible.[15] For all that, I am not yet a disciple.[16] We lack many things [we still need]

---

13 *zelos* ("envy"). This is usually translated "jealousy" or "zeal." Here Ignatius clearly sees it as a vice to be countered by humility and meekness. *Zelos* in context is a vice for which suffering is the cure. Evil is destroyed by its opposite, meekness (*praotes*).

14 In his typically self-deprecating manner Ignatius has great confidence in God but knows his own weakness and limitations. He knows that suffering engenders humility and meekness while others praising him may be his downfall. Here the heart of Ignatius as a servant of God stands in the foreground.

15 The enumeration of heavenly powers is reflected in Smyrn 6:1 and in Paul Eph 1:20,21 and Col 1:16 where Christ is above all heavenly powers.

16 Almost all translations take the "not" with the statement "I am not a disciple," but the Greek text could be translated other ways. I have followed the traditional translation because elsewhere Ignatius speaks of himself as not yet being a disciple. See Eph 3:1 and Rom 5:3.

so that we may not lack God himself.

Chapter 6

(1) I appeal to you, not I, but the love of Jesus Christ. Use only Christian food and abstain from a foreign plant that is heresy. (2) Those who appear worthy of trust[17] mingle Jesus Christ with themselves.[18] It is like someone giving a deadly poison with honey-wine. The one who receives this very thing with a sweet taste ends up dying of an evil desire.

Chapter 7

(1) Guard against such people. This will be [true] for you when you are not puffed up and are inseparable from God, i.e. Jesus Christ, the bishop, and the orders of the apostles.[19] (2) The one who is within the altar is pure; the one outside the altar is not pure, that is, the one who does something without the bishop and the presbytery and the deacons. This person is not pure in conscience.[20]

---

17 *kataxiopisteuomenoi* ("who appear worthy of trust") is difficult to translate here. Ehrman has "such persons seem to be trustworthy" while Camelot has "those who attempt to pass themselves off as worthy of the faith."

18 Camelot adds "with their error" rather than "with themselves." This chapter speaks of Christian teaching as food. In contrast to those who mix the message of Christ with their own doctrines, Ignatius urges the consumption of truth flowing from "the love of Jesus Christ." Like Paul, the bishop of Antioch sees doctrinal purity and personal love as twin sisters.

19 "orders of the apostles." This expression shows not only that Ignatius himself has apostolic authority (see comment on the salutation) but that the bishop and his presbyters function with apostolic authority.

20 7:2 shows how intimately purity, sacrament, and sacrifice are intertwined in Ignatius. Some scholars think Ignatius means ritual purity as in the OT but this is a modern distinction between moral and ritual purity. For Ignatius and later fathers of the church, moral purity could come from ritual purity because the Christian altar had the Lamb of God who brings purity to human beings. The

Chapter 8

(1) I have not known any such thing among you but I caution you who are my beloved because I foresee the treachery of the devil. So, by seizing upon gentleness, create yourselves anew in faith which is the flesh of the Lord, and in love which is the blood of Christ.[21] (2) Let none of you hold something against his neighbor. Do not give opportunities to the pagans so that the congregation[22] in God may not be blasphemed on account of a few foolish people. Woe to him through whom some blaspheme my name in futility.[23]

Chapter 9

(1) So play the deaf-mute when anyone speaks to you without Jesus Christ who was from David's tribe, from Mary, who was truly born, ate, and drank, was truly persecuted in the time of Pontius Pilate, truly was crucified and died while the [powers] of heaven, of earth, and under the earth looked on.[24] (2) He was truly raised from the dead by his Father raising him. The Father, that is, the Father in Christ Jesus, will raise us who

---

Eucharist, because it contains the sacrifice of Christ on Calvary, purifies those who are "within the altar."

21 "recreate yourselves, etc." Ignatius teaches the renewal of the inner life of the soul with God through the sacrament of the Eucharist. Fighting against false teaching requires fortification in gentleness, faith, and love. These virtues are given by God through the flesh and blood of Christ who is the perfect embodiment of them. For a discussion of the Eucharist and spiritual nourishment, see Camelot, p. 46. Lightfoot reads *anaktesas* "recover, refresh."

22 Ignatius uses *plethos* for "congregation."

23 An allusion to Is 52:5.

24 "while the [powers] of heaven." Ignatius here reflects the Pauline theme of the cosmic significance of Christ's life, death, and resurrection. See Paul Phil 2:5-11.

believe in him in like manner. Without him we do not have true life.

Chapter 10

(1) Now if some who are without God, that is unbelievers, claim he only seemed to have suffered — they are ones for whom the language of appearance is appropriate — then why am I a prisoner and why do I desire to fight with beasts? If it were true, there would be no point to my death.[25] I would be bearing false witness against the Lord.

Chapter 11

(1) Flee from evil offshoots that give birth only to death-bearing fruit. If anyone tastes this he dies at once. These are not the Father's plantings. (2) If they were, they would appear as branches of the cross and their fruit would be incorruptible. Through it, in his passion, he calls you his members. Therefore, the head cannot be born without members since God promises that unity which is himself.[26]

Chapter 12

(1) I greet you from Smyrna together with the churches of God that are present with me. These are those who have refreshed me in flesh and spirit in every way. (2) My chains that

---

25 *dorean* ("no point ") can also mean "freely" and so could be translated "I die of my own free will."

26 Unity within the church is not only external obedience to the bishop but is a real union between Christ the head and believers as the members. This union is accomplished through the passion and cross. This text reflects Paul's doctrine of the church as the mystical body (see Paul Eph 5:23,30). Ignatius's botanical imagery also seems to draw on Jesus's words in Jn 15:1-15 about the vine and the branches.

I carry for the sake of Jesus Christ appeal to you[27] as I ask to attain to God. Stay in your harmony and in your prayer with one another. It is fitting for each of you, particularly the presbyters, to bring refreshment to the bishop for the honor of the Father of Jesus Christ and of the apostles. (3) I appeal to you in love to listen to me that by my writing I may not be a witness in your midst.[28] Now pray for me as I need the love [emanating] from you in the mercy of God[29] to make me worthy of the lot[30] which I am set to obtain. Pray that I may not be found unapproved.[31]

Chapter 13

(1) The love of the Smyrneans and Ephesians greets you. Remember the church in Syria in your prayers. I am not even worthy to claim to be the least of these.[32] (2) Farewell in Jesus Christ. Be subject to the bishop as you are to the commandment; and likewise to the presbytery. Love each and every one with an undivided heart. (3) My spirit makes you pure[33] not

---

27 *parakalei humas* ("appeal to you") may also be translated "encourage you."

28 "that I may not be a witness in your midst," i.e. to condemn them by their failure to follow Ignatius's commands.

29 "as I need the love [emanating] from you." Ignatius here expresses how the love of Christians shared in the mystical body prepares each member for fulfilling his vocation, which is the call to martyrdom.

30 *kleros* ("lot") became the normal word for "clergy" in late Christian Greek. In this context the most natural reading is that Ignatius means the destiny of martyrdom though he may also be thinking of the inheritance of the Saints in heaven.

31 Ignatius uses Paul's language from 1 Cor 9:27.

32 Though the bishop of Antioch, Ignatius sees himself as the least of the faithful. Though this may appear to be pious exaggeration for the sake of effect, holy priests often view themselves simply as the lowest of the lowly recalling Christ's instruction to his apostles (Mk 10:35-45). A bishop, when he prays the liturgy, is reminded in the prayers themselves that he is only God's "unworthy servant."

33 "My spirit makes you pure" is translated variously as "my own spirit is sacrificed

only now but also when I attain to God.[34] I am still under danger but the Father is faithful in Jesus Christ to fulfill my and your request. May you be found blameless in him!

---

for you" (Ehrman, Camelot), and "My spirit is devoted to you" (Lightfoot). *Hagnizo* is used in the NT (see 1 Jn 3:5; 1 Pet 1:22) to mean "purify, cleanse, make pure." There seems no reason not to take it in that sense here. I have read it as a middle voice "makes you pure" but it could be the passive "my spirit is made pure by you" or even "my spirit makes yours (i.e. spirit) pure."

34 Ignatius implies that his prayers and merits derived from Christ will benefit the Trallians even after his death. The intercession of the Saints is rooted in the rich Pauline teaching of communion in the mystical body of Christ (i.e. the church).

Chapter Ten
Ignatius's Letter to the Romans Translation and Commentary

The *Letter to the Romans* is the only one of the seven letters not addressed to a church or bishop of Asia Minor. Since Ignatius was en route to Rome to face his martyrdom, he appeals to the Roman Christians not to hinder his opportunity to share in the passion of Christ. His address to the Roman church contains descriptions and praises of the church there which are not found in any of his other six letters. Of this church alone he says that it "presides in love" and "presides in the region of the Romans." Unlike the letters to the Smyrneans or to the Philadelphians, Ignatius does not comment on the eucharistic liturgy but he draws on the same theme to speak of his own desire to be "the wheat of God" (4:1) and to have "the bread of God that is the flesh of Jesus Christ" (7:2). For Ignatius, Eucharist and martyrdom lead to the same reality of possessing Jesus Christ.

Salutation

Ignatius, called Theophorus, to the church that receives mercy in the majesty of the Father Most High and of Jesus Christ his only Son. This church has been loved and enlightened in the will of him who willed all things that exist in accord with the faith and love of Jesus Christ, our God. Your church presides in the region of the Romans;[1] it is worthy of God, worthy of propriety, worthy of blessing, worthy of praise, worthy of success, worthy of purity, and presiding in love, named by Christ, named by the Father.[2] I greet your church in the name of Jesus Christ, the Father's Son. To you who are united in flesh and spirit to his every command, filled with God's grace without distinction, and strained off from every foreign color, especially in Jesus Christ, our God, I give greetings blamelessly.

Chapter 1

(1) Since I asked God in prayer I obtained the privilege of seeing your God-worthy faces as I sought to receive them

---

1   *hetis kai prokathetai in topo choriou Romaion* ("your church presides in the region of the Romans") has been taken in two ways, one of which supports the claim to papal primacy. Camelot notes that the text says "in the region of the Romans," not "over the region of the Romans." What is implied is that in the region where it is established, the church of Rome presides. But presides over what? The other interpretation simply notes that we have here one more expression of praise along with the other attributes mentioned by Ignatius and does not necessarily ascribe any special power to the church of Rome. For a fuller discussion, see chapter 4.

2   The nine attributes of the Roman church listed here are unique among the letters even though other letters do contain praises for the churches. The greater extent of praise for the church in Rome fits well with the statement that this church presides over other churches.

even more. In being bound as a prisoner in Christ Jesus, I hope to greet you if in fact it may be his will for us to be counted worthy to arrive at this end. (2) Indeed, the beginning is well-established if in fact I attain the grace for me to receive my share unimpeded. I am somewhat afraid of your love lest it do me wrong. For you it is easy to do whatever you want. It is hard for me to reach God unless you spare me.[3]

Chapter 2

(1) I do not want you to please people but God, as you are pleasing God. As for me, I will not have such a singular opportunity[4] to reach God. And you, unless you remain silent, will not be able to be inscribed in a better work.[5] For if you remain silent about me, I will become God's but if you love my flesh, I will be running again.[6] (2) Do not prevent me from being poured out to God as a libation when there is still an altar that you may be a chorus in love, singing to the Father in Christ Jesus since God counted the bishop of Syria to be found worthy of being sent from east to west. It is good that I should be like the sun setting from this world so that I may rise to God.

---

3 Ignatius is afraid that their love for him will prevent his martyrdom in Rome. He urges them not to allow their noble intentions to get in the way of his obtaining his share in glory.

4 *kairos* ("singular opportunity"): a moment of time that often connotes opportunity.

5 Ignatius sees the Roman Christians' cooperation in his martyrdom as contributing to their salvation. The reference to their being inscribed probably alludes to the "book of life" mentioned in Rev 13:8.

6 Some MSS have *phone* ("sound") instead of *trechon* ("running"). Thus Ehrman translates "I will once again be a mere noise."

Chapter 3

(1) You never deceived anyone; you have taught others. I want those things to be firm which, once learned, you taught. (2) Only ask that I may have the power, not only to speak outwardly, but to desire inwardly to be called a Christian and [in fact] be found to be one. If I am truly found one, I will be able to be called one and then be faithful when I no longer make my appearance in this world. (3) Nothing that simply appears is good. Our God, Jesus Christ, rather was manifested as being truly in the Father. The matter is not a matter of persuasion but Christianity partakes of greatness when it is hated by the world.[7]

Chapter 4

(1) I write and command all the churches that I willingly die for God, if in fact you do not prevent me. I appeal to you not to be inopportune even with a noble purpose. Permit me to be food for the beasts; through them I will reach God. I am the wheat of God[8] and I compete through the beasts' teeth to be found the pure bread of Christ.[9] (2) Rather flatter[10] the

---

7   Chapter 3 signals an important part of Ignatius's teaching. The Docetists constantly used the word "appear" in their speech. To this Ignatius contrasts the reality of Christ being in the Father. In the same way, the true disciple is not interested in appearances; he is concerned about being a true follower of Christ. Only then will the Christian truly appear to be what he is, Jesus's disciple.

8   See also Rom 7:2.

9   Eucharist and martyrdom are intimately related. Through receiving Christ in the Eucharist a person becomes more and more a disciple of Christ. The love that grows in the heart through sacramental communion makes a disciple desire to be with Christ, a reality afforded by martyrdom. The martyr's heart then finds its fulfillment in full union with Jesus Christ in which he becomes the same reality he receives in the Eucharist and so can be called the bread of God.

10 *kolakeuo* ("flatter") can mean "entice" or "charm." Ignatius imagines the Roman Christians to be much like a bullfighter who entices a bull to charge.

beasts to become my tomb and to leave nothing of my body that by dying I may not be a burden to you. Then I will be truly a disciple of Jesus Christ when the world will not even see my body. Beg Christ in my behalf that I may be found a sacrifice to God through these instruments. (3) I do not command you as Peter and Paul did.[11] They were apostles; I am a criminal. They were free but I am a slave even now. Rather, if I suffer I will be liberated for Jesus Christ and I will rise again free in him. For now I am learning as a prisoner to desire nothing else.

Chapter 5

(1) I do battle with beasts from Syria to Rome, by land and by sea, night and day, having been bound to ten leopards, that is, to the military detachment.[12] In fact, those who are receiving kindness become worse. In their injustices, I am becoming more of a disciple, "but I am not justified because of this."[13] (2) May I profit from the beasts prepared for me and I ask that the time be shortened. The beasts I entice I hope will devour me quickly and not, as in some cases, when they are too cowardly to touch [their victims]. If they are unwilling to touch me, I will force them. Grant me this; I myself know what is good for me. (3) Just now I am beginning to be a

---

11 This text has sometimes been interpreted as Ignatius's denial of his own apostolic authority (so Bauer), but the contrast here is not between two different types of authority, one apostolic and the other sub-apostolic. Ignatius is contrasting the apostles with his own criminal condition. For a fuller explanation, see chapter 4.

12 "detachment" is lit. "order" (*tagma*).

13 See 1 Cor 4:4.

disciple so that I am zealous for nothing visible or invisible[14] that I may reach Jesus Christ. Let it all come upon me: fire and cross, fierceness of beasts, being cut up, torn apart, breaking of bones, beating of members, grinding of the whole body, torments of the devil. Only this remains: I desire to reach Jesus Christ.

Chapter 6

(1) Neither the pleasures of this world nor the kingdoms of this age will profit me. It is good for me to die for Jesus Christ,[15] or to reign over the ends of the earth.[16] I seek him who died for us. I want him who rose for our sake. My birth lies before me.[17] (2) Brothers, agree with me. Do not bind me to this life. Do not wish me to die.[18] Do not give the world one who wants God[19] nor try to deceive me with material things. Permit me to receive a pure light. By arriving there I will be truly human.[20] (3) Permit

---

14 "so that I am zealous for nothing visible or invisible." Camelot, Ehrman, and Holmes take this phrase as a wish, whereas I have translated it as a result clause following from Ignatius's statement of being a disciple. The more he becomes a disciple of Christ, the less the world attracts Ignatius.

15 Or "that my death leads to Jesus Christ." Ignatius uses an aorist infinitive for "to die" which connotes a finality to the death he is imagining.

16 Dying for Jesus Christ will make Ignatius reign with him in heaven.

17 Ignatius initiates the practice of ancient Christians who spoke of the day of their death as their birthday to eternal life. The church chooses the day of a Saint's death as the preferred day of his or her feast.

18 This sentence could be translated as a question expecting a negative answer: "You don't wish me to die, do you?" (i.e. don't wish me to die to eternal life by staying here in this world).

19 Or it could be translated, "one who wants to be God's."

20 Ignatius here uses the word *anthropos* which means "man" in a generic sense (i.e. mankind, cf. anthropology). The word *aner* means man as male. Here Ignatius is expressing the firm Christian idea that to be with God is to be fully human, a concept that Irenaeus of Lyons will later express as "the glory of God is man fully alive." His idea contrasts with the world of Greek mythology which says that to

me to be an imitator of the sufferings of my God. If anyone possesses him in himself, let him consider what I want and let him suffer with me because he understands the things that compel me.[21]

Chapter 7

(1) The ruler of this world wishes to tear me into pieces and to corrupt my yearning[22] for God. Let none of you who are present help him. Rather be mine, or better, be God's. Do not talk about Jesus Christ and desire the world at the same time. Let no deception dwell among you. (2) And while I am not present, I exhort you. Be persuaded by me, or rather, be persuaded by the things that I write to you. While I am alive, I write to you but I desire death. My desire [for this world] has been crucified and there is no fire in me burning for material things. Water is living and speaking in me, speaking from within.[23] Come to the Father.[24] I have no desire for corruptible food or for the pleasures of this life. I want the bread of God that is the flesh of Jesus Christ, of David's seed, and I

---

become like the gods, one must become less human and to become more fully human, one must become less divine. Our humanity is at its fullest when we are full of God. The later Greek fathers expressed the same notion by the term *theosis* or divinization.

21 Rom 6:3 draws on Paul's theology of suffering. Entering into the sufferings of Christ is the means by which we come to possess him more completely (cf. Col 1:24; Phil 3:10).

22 *gnome* ("yearning") has a wide range of meanings. It could also refer more to Ignatius's faith than to his emotion.

23 Ignatius is almost certainly alluding to the waters of baptism. The water of baptism douses the fire of passion in the human soul. It also alludes to Jesus's words in Jn 4:10,14; 7:37-39.

24 See Jn 14:12ff.

want his blood as my drink that is love incorruptible.[25]

Chapter 8

(1) I no longer want to live a purely human life. And this will be the case if you desire it. May you desire it that you may be desired! I appeal to you by a few letters. (2) Believe me. Jesus Christ will show you that I speak in truth. He is the mouth without a lie in whom the Father speaks truly. (3) Ask that I may obtain it. I wrote to you not according to human desire[26] but according to God's will. If I suffer, it is because you have desired it. If I am rejected, it is because you hated me.

Chapter 9

(1) Remember the church in Syria in your prayer that uses God as their shepherd instead of me. Jesus Christ alone will watch over it as well as your love.[27] (2) I am ashamed to even speak of them for I am not worthy to do so since I am the least of them and a miscarriage.[28] But I received mercy to be

---

25 Chapter 7 draws heavily on Ignatius's sacramental theology which teaches that the possession of love in the Christian heart comes from Christ's fleshly presence in the Eucharist. The heaven Ignatius desires will afford him the true substance of Christ's flesh and blood, namely, to be nourished forever on the humanity and divinity of Christ in the beatific vision. The context also suggests that as love for the Eucharist grows, love for the present world diminishes.

26 Lit. "according to the flesh."

27 The word "alone" applies only to Jesus Christ but Ignatius adds "your love" because by loving the church of Syria through prayer the Roman Christians participate in Christ's shepherding of the Antiochean church. This language is part of the Pauline idea of how members of the body of Christ share in the ministry of Christ over the church.

28 *ektroma* ("miscarriage") means "abortion" in a medical context. Ignatius uses it here as an expression of humility as does Paul in 1 Cor 15:8 where it is usually translated "born out of time." The Antiochean father may be imitating Paul's humble expression.

someone if I can reach God. (3) My spirit and the love of the churches who received me in the name of Jesus Christ greet you. They did not receive me as a passer-by. For even those churches which did not fit into my path in my human plans advanced my journey in each city.

Chapter 10

(1) I write you these things from Smyrna through the Ephesians who are most worthy of blessing. Crocus is here with me along with many others. His name is beloved to me. (2) About those who have preceded me from Syria to Rome, I believe you have recognized them. Tell them that I am close for they are all worthy of God and of you. It is appropriate for you to give them rest in every way. (3) I wrote you these things before the ninth calends of September. Farewell till the end in the patience[29] of Jesus Christ.

---

29 *hupomone* ("patience)" can mean "endurance;" i.e. the endurance which takes us to the day of Christ's return.

Chapter Eleven
Ignatius's Letter to the Philadelphians
Translation and Commentary

Ignatius wrote this letter from Troas (11:2) after he had left Smyrna. The church in Philadelphia is addressed in Rev 3:7-13 where it is evident that there was a strong clash between Jews and Christians. In chapter 6, Ignatius speaks of the same conflict by using the terms Judaism and Christianity in a way that never occurs in the New Testament. The same problem clearly lies behind both documents. By Ignatius's time, Christians had become distinct enough that Jews probably no longer thought of Jewish Christians as Jews. Whatever the precise nature of the conflict, Ignatius urges the Philadelphians to come together around one Eucharist in obedience to their bishop (4:1) because his office derives from divine appointment (1:1). For him, Christ is the fulfillment of the promises of the old covenant (9:1,2). Like the author of the *Letter to the Hebrews*, Ignatius exhorts his readers to embrace the fullness of faith in Christ.

Salutation

Ignatius, called Theophorus, to the church of God the Father and of the Lord Jesus Christ that is in Philadelphia of Asia. This church has received mercy, has been established in the harmony of God, and rejoices in the suffering of our Lord unquestionably, and is fully confident in his mercy in his resurrection. I greet this church in the blood of Jesus Christ, a church that is eternal and abiding joy,[1] especially if they are at one with the bishop, with his presbyters, and the deacons who have been approved in the mind of Jesus Christ. He established them by his very own will in confirmation through his Holy Spirit.

Chapter 1

(1) I knew that this bishop did not obtain his ministry for the common good from himself or by human approval or by vainglory but rather in the love of God the Father and of the Lord Jesus Christ.[2] I am amazed at his gentleness. Even when silent, he is able to do more than those who speak futile things. (2) He is well tuned to the commandments as a lyre to strings. For this reason, my soul blesses his mindfulness of God[3] because I know he is virtuous and perfect; I know his steadfastness and freedom from anger in the

---

1 "church that is eternal and abiding joy." It is not clear what the relative pronoun "that" refers to. Holmes translates it "which is eternal and lasting joy" referring the pronoun to the blood of Christ but the pronoun is feminine and "blood" is neuter in Greek. Bauer follows my translation by referring the pronoun to the church which is feminine.

2 Ignatius's praise of the episcopal office may be inspired by Paul's reference to the divine source of his own vocation as an apostle in Gal 1:1.

3 *ten eis theon autou gnomen* ("mindfulness of God") may also be translated "his mind directed toward God" (Bauer, Camelot), or "his godly mind" (Holmes).

gentleness of the living God.[4]

Chapter 2

(1) As children of the light of truth, flee division and evil teaching. Where the Shepherd is, there you should follow like sheep.[5] (2) Many wolves, who can be trustworthy when it comes to evil pleasure, want to enslave those who run after God but they have no place in your unity.[6]

Chapter 3

(1) Abstain from evil plants which Jesus Christ does not cultivate because they are not the Father's planting. (2) Not that I have found division among you but rather a filter.[7] As many as belong to God and to Jesus Christ, these are with the bishop. Let those who have repented come to the unity of the church, and these belong to God that they may live in accord with Jesus Christ. (3) Do not be deceived, my brothers! If someone follows a schismatic, he will not inherit the kingdom

---

4 Ignatius stresses that the bishop as a shepherd of the church must display those virtues which reflect Christ himself. Most important is *epieikeia* ("gentleness" or "flexibility"). Paul uses this word in 2 Cor 10:1, "through the meekness and gentleness of Christ." While Ignatius fully endorses the divine authority of the bishop's office, he does not conceive of its exercise as authoritarian. The shepherd of God's flock must be patient and gentle above all.

5 "Shepherd." Does this refer to Christ as the Shepherd of the sheep (Jn 10:11) or to the bishops as human shepherds? The text can be read either way or perhaps both.

6 Ehrman and Holmes translate "trustworthy" as "seemingly trustworthy" but Ignatius may be speaking ironically, i.e. wolves dressed in sheep's clothing can be trusted to do evil but will destroy God's flock if they can. The imagery of shepherd, sheep, and wolves finds precedent in Scripture (Mt 7:15). Here Ignatius stresses that true shepherds like Christ are always concerned with the unity of the church.

7 I.e. to distinguish the faithful from false believers.

of God. If someone walks in a strange mind set, he is not consenting to the Passion.[8]

Chapter 4

(1) So be diligent to use one Eucharist for there is [only] one flesh of our Lord Jesus Christ and one cup for unity in his blood. There is one altar as there is one bishop together with his presbyters, and deacons, my fellow servants. This is so that whatever you do, you may do in accord with God.[9]

Chapter 5

(1) My brothers, I am being completely poured out for love of you and with exceeding joy I try to make you secure. It is really not I but Jesus Christ who does so. In him, as a prisoner, I am all the more afraid because I am still incomplete. However, your prayer will make me complete for God so that I may obtain a share in that lot where I have received mercy. I flee for refuge in the gospel like I do in the flesh of Jesus and in the apostles as in the presbytery of the church. (2) We love the prophets because they announced the gospel, hoped in him and waited for him. They were saved by their faith because they were in the unity of Jesus Christ.[10] Being holy, they were worthy of love

---

8   Here Ignatius uses *pathos* without modifiers but it clearly refers to Christ's suffering on the cross. Holding to doctrines or opinions out of accord with the apostolic faith places one in opposition to Christ's suffering because the preaching of the apostles centered on the cross (see 1 Cor 2:2).

9   See chapter 5 in the introductory essays for a discussion of the meaning of chapter 4 in the letter. The emphasis on the "oneness" of the Eucharist implies that there may have been an alternative church or liturgy at Philadelphia. The reason for Ignatius stressing "one Eucharist" is also because the faithful must know where they can find the true flesh and blood of Jesus Christ.

10   "in the unity of Jesus Christ" probably means that the OT prophets were in

and of wonder, and they were witnessed by Jesus Christ and were numbered in the gospel of our common hope.

Chapter 6

(1) If anyone tries to interpret Judaism for you, do not listen to him. It is better to hear about Christianity from a man who has circumcision than about Judaism from an uncircumcised man.[11] But if neither of them speaks about Jesus Christ, to me they are grave stones and tombs of the dead on which only the names of men are inscribed. (2) Flee the evil practices[12] and snares of the ruler of this age lest you grow weak in love by his troubling of your mind. Rather, come together in an undivided heart. (3) I thank my God that I have a clear conscience among you and that no one can boast secretly or in public that I have burdened anyone in ways small or great. I ask all to whom I spoke not to hold it as a witness against themselves.[13]

Chapter 7

(1) If some wanted to deceive me according to the flesh, the Spirit is not deceived because it is from God. For he knows from where he comes and where he is going and he exposes the secret things. I cried out when I was in your midst; I spoke with a loud voice, the voice of God, "pay attention to the bishop, to

---

union with Christ even though they lived before him and never saw him.

11 Ignatius uses the language of circumcision from the OT to declare that it is the Christian who is truly circumcised. His usage has precedents in Col 2:12,13 where Paul suggests that baptism is equivalent to the circumcision of the old covenant.

12 See comment on Polyc 5:1.

13 I.e. that the words Ignatius spoke when in Philadelphia will not come back to haunt those who opposed him.

the presbytery, and to the deacons." There are some who mistrusted me that I said these things as if I knew beforehand of the division caused by some. But he is my witness in whom I am bound that I knew nothing from a human source.[14] (2) The Spirit proclaimed it thus: do nothing without the bishop, keep your flesh as a temple of God, love unity, spurn divisions, become imitators of Jesus Christ as he is of the Father.

Chapter 8

(1) I was acting on my own as a man prepared for unity. Where there is division and wrath, God does not dwell there. The Lord forgives all who repent if their repentance leads back to God's unity[15] and the council of the bishop. I believe in the grace of Jesus Christ who will free you from every bond. (2) I appeal to you to practice nothing from a spirit of factionalism but only what you learned from Christ. I heard some saying that "if I did not find [these things] among the ancients, I do not believe it in the gospel." I said to them, "it is written." For me, Jesus Christ is ancient. His cross, death, and resurrection are the ancient archives.[16] So too is the faith that comes through him in which I wish to be justified in your prayer.[17]

---

14 *kata sarka*, lit. "according to the flesh."

15 I.e. to the unity God established and continues to provide in the church.

16 *athikta* ("the ancient archives") are the saving events of the Paschal Mystery which become the criterion to distinguish truth and error. The Jews in Philadelphia may have been arguing that the Christian claims about Jesus Christ were not found in the history of Israel or in the Hebrew Scriptures.

17 Holmes and Ehrman take "faith" as *fides qua creditur* (subjective) while it may very well be *fides quae creditur*, i.e. the objective content of the faith.

Chapter 9

(1) Priests[18] are fine but the high priest who has been entrusted with the holy of holies is better. He alone has been entrusted with the secret things of God. He himself is the door of the Father[19] through which Abraham, Isaac, Jacob, the prophets, the apostles, and the church enter. These things are designed to lead to God's unity.[20] (2) The gospel contains something excellent: the coming of the Savior, our Lord Jesus Christ, his suffering, and resurrection. The beloved prophets made their proclamations with a view to him. The gospel is the perfection of immortality. Everything together is beautiful if you hold your faith in love.[21]

Chapter 10

(1) Since it has been told me that the church in Antioch of Syria is at peace by your prayer and the compassion you have in Christ Jesus, it is fitting for you to elect a deacon to send him there as an ambassador of God so that you may share their joy in a common bond[22] and give glory to the name [of God]. (2) Blessed in Jesus Christ is he who will be counted worthy of this ministry. You too will be honored. To you who wish to do it, it is not impossible in behalf of God's name since some closer churches have sent bishops while

---

18 "Priests," i.e. of the old covenant. Jesus Christ is the true high priest, an idea taken from the *Letter to the Hebrews*. See 4:14; 7:1ff; 9:11-14.

19 See Jn 10:7,9.

20 See comment on 8:1.

21 *ean en agape pisteuete* ("if you hold your faith in love"). Ehrman has "if you believe while showing love." Holmes has "if you believe with love."

22 *epi to auto* ("in a common bond") could mean several things. Ehrman has "achieve a common purpose." Holmes has "when they have assembled together." All these translations are legitimate.

others sent presbyters and deacons.

Chapter 11

(1) Now about Philo, the deacon from Cilicia, a well-proven man, who serves me in the word of God with Rheus Agathopous, a chosen man, who followed me from Syria after renouncing this life. These give witness about you and I thank God for you because you received them as the Lord received you. May those who dishonored them be redeemed in the grace of Jesus Christ! (2) The love of the brothers and sisters in Troas greets you. So I write you through Burrhus who was sent with me by the Ephesians and Smyrneans as a matter of honor. The Lord Jesus Christ will honor them. In him they have placed their hope in flesh, spirit, faith, love, harmony. Farewell in Christ Jesus, our shared hope.

Chapter Twelve
Ignatius's Letter to the Smyrneans
Translation and Commentary

The church at Smyrna and its bishop Polycarp were especially dear to Ignatius. Of all the cities and communities of Asia Minor he chose Smyrna as his main stopping-off point en route to Rome. Along with the following letter to Polycarp (see chapter 13), this letter to the church itself indicates that those troubles facing the other churches were also present in Smyrna. John the Seer also wrote a short letter to the church at Smyrna (Rev 2:8-11) from which we infer that there must have been quite a clash between Jews and Gentile Christians there as in Philadelphia. We can infer from Ignatius's letter that the heresy threatening the church in Smyrna was some form of Docetism (3:1-3) fueled by some claim to visions and private revelations. In this letter too we learn that the denial of a real Incarnation of the Son of God led to its natural consequence, i.e. the denial of the humanity of Jesus in the Eucharist (7:1).

Salutation

Ignatius, called Theophorus, to the church of God the Father and of his beloved Jesus Christ. Your church in Smyrna of Asia has received mercy in every gracious gift, fulfilled in faith and love, not lacking in any gift, most worthy of God, and bearing holiness. Greetings in the blameless Spirit and Word of God.

Chapter 1

(1) I glorify Jesus Christ, the God who made you wise, for I know that you have been prepared in an unshakable faith, as you were nailed to the cross of the Lord Jesus Christ in flesh and spirit and established in love in the blood of Christ, having been fulfilled for our Lord. He is truly from the tribe of David according to the flesh, but the Son of God according to the will and power of God, truly born of a virgin, baptized by John that all righteousness may be fulfilled by him.[1] (2) Truly he was nailed [to the cross] in the flesh for us under Pontius Pilate and Herod the tetrarch — we received from the fruit of his divinely blessed suffering — that he might carry the banner[2] for the ages through the resurrection for his holy and faithful ones, whether Jew or Gentile, in the one body of his church.

Chapter 2

(1) He suffered all these things for us to be saved. And truly he suffered as he also truly raised himself. It is not like some

---

1   An allusion to Mt 3:13-17.

2   s*ussemon* ("banner"), i.e. a battle standard such as the Roman armies carried. Ignatius seems to allude to Is 5:26 but here conceives of the cross as the banner which leads the army of God (cf. the church militant).

unbelievers say, that he only seemed to suffer.[3] They are ones who only seem to be. It will happen to them as they imagine since they will be bodiless and demonic.[4]

Chapter 3

(1) I for one know and believe that he was in the flesh after the resurrection. (2) When he came to those around Peter, he said to them, "Take, handle me and see that I am not an incorporeal spirit."[5] Immediately they touched and believed in him, being mingled with his flesh and spirit.[6] For this reason they too despised death and were found to be above death. (3) After the resurrection he ate and drank with them as a fleshly being even though he was spiritually united to the Father.[7]

Chapter 4

(1) These are the things I warn you about even though I know that you hold them. I am protecting you in advance from the beasts in human form. Not only should you not receive them; if possible you should not meet with them. Rather, pray

---

3   The Docetists in Tralles also used the language of appearance.

4   Later Christian authors speak about the damned as bodiless demons. See Camelot p. 134.

5   *daimonion* ("an incorporeal spirit"), usually translated demon in the NT, is also used in Greek to mean any spirit, good or bad.

6   Perhaps the story of Thomas the apostle is in Ignatius's mind. See Jn 20:24-29 where Jesus appeared to him. The phrase "mingled with his flesh and spirit" in some MSS is "mingled with his flesh and blood." The choice of the verb "mingle" may allude to the Eucharist. As many fathers will later say, the one who receives the flesh and blood of Christ in the sacrament is as truly united and mingled with Christ as those who accompanied him during his earthly pilgrimage.

7   This insistence on Jesus being bodily present to the apostles is emphasized by Paul in 1 Cor 15:3-8.

for them that somehow they may repent even if it is difficult.[8] Jesus Christ, our true life, has authority over this. (2) If these things only seemed to be done by the Lord, then I only seem to have been bound. Why have I surrendered myself to death, to fire, to the sword, to beasts? However, near the sword is near to God; to be among the beasts is to be in God[9] when it is in the name of Jesus Christ. I endure all things to suffer with him. He who became the perfect man strengthens me.[10]

Chapter 5

(1) Some deny him in ignorance, or rather, are denied by him since they are advocates of death more than of the truth. Neither the prophets nor Moses persuaded them. (2) But even now neither the gospel nor our human sufferings have persuaded them. They think the same thing about us. What profit does anyone give me if he praises me but blasphemes my Lord by refusing to confess that he bears flesh? The one who does not say this [happened] has completely denied him since he is a carrier of death. (3) It did not seem to me [appropriate] to

---

8   Ignatius is referring specifically to repentance with respect to the church and its unity. See Philad 3:2; 8:1, and below Smyrn 5:3.

9   "to be among the beasts is to be in God." To bring Ignatius's Greek into English at this point is difficult. Ehrman has "to be in the presence of the wild beasts is to be in the presence of God" and Holmes has "with the beasts means with God." The preposition *metaxu* means "in between" or "among" (cf. Latin *inter*). Ignatius uses *metaxu* with both beasts and God but he is drawing on the wider range of meaning implicit in the word. *Metaxu therion* means "among the beasts" but it sounds strange in English to say "among God." However, Ignatius is saying that to be among the beasts puts the victim inside the very heart of God. Here is another of Ignatius's ways of stressing suffering as a means of drawing near to God.

10   See Paul in Phil 4:13.

inscribe their names since they are unbelievers. However, may it never be mine even to remember them until they turn back to the passion which is our resurrection.[11]

Chapter 6

(1) Let no one be deceived. If the heavenly powers, the glory of angels, and the visible and invisible rulers do not believe in the blood of Christ,[12] judgment awaits them. Let the one who can receive this do so. Position should not cause anyone to boast. Faith and love are the whole matter and nothing should be judged about this in advance. (2) You have noted those who teach heterodox things about the grace of Jesus Christ which came to us. How they are contrary to the mind of God! They are not concerned about love, neither the widow, the orphan, the afflicted — whether bound or free, the hungry nor the thirsty.

Chapter 7

(1) They abstain from the Eucharist and from [set times of] prayer because they do not confess that the Eucharist is the flesh of our Savior Jesus Christ, that flesh which suffered for our sins but which the Father raised in his kindness.[13] Those who

---

11 Here Ignatius shows how intimately the sufferings and resurrection are two parts of the one Paschal Mystery. Embracing the sufferings of Christ is inextricably bound up with his resurrection. One cannot be had without the other. Again, Ignatius shows himself to be imbued with the central truths of Paul's theology, i.e. union with Christ in his death and resurrection.

12 What does it mean to "not believe in the blood of Christ?" It certainly refers to the saving efficacy of his bloody death on the cross. In the light of what Ignatius says in chapter 7, it probably also means that they should believe in his blood in the Eucharist to be saved.

13 In keeping with what was said in 6:1, Ignatius now insists on the real human

contradict the gift of God with strife will die. It would have been more profitable for them to love that they may also rise [again]. (2) It is proper to avoid such people and not to speak about them in private or in public. Rather, it is profitable to hold to the prophets, and especially to the gospel in which the passion has been shown us and the resurrection completed. It is these divisions which you should flee as the beginning of evils.[14]

Chapter 8

(1) You all should follow the bishop as Jesus Christ does the Father. Follow too the presbytery as the apostles, and honor the deacons as the command of God. Let no one do anything that is proper for the church without the bishop. Let that Eucharist be considered valid that is under the bishop or performed by one to whom he entrusts it. (2) Wherever the bishop appears, let there be the fullness [of the church] as wherever Christ Jesus appears, there is the catholic church.[15] It is not lawful to baptize or to hold an agape feast without the bishop.[16] On the other hand, what he

---

(fleshly) presence of Jesus in the Eucharist. For a fuller explanation of this passage, see the essay on the Eucharist in chapter 5.

14 In some MSS this sentence begins chapter 8.

15 Here is the earliest known occurrence of the phrase "catholic church," though Ignatius uses it as if it were already a standard term rather than his own creation. This, of course, is one of the four marks of the church that will later be expressed in the Nicene creed: "I believe in one, holy, catholic, and apostolic church." The word *katholikos* ("catholic") means universal and describes an essential feature of the church Christ founded. Christ intended the church to be for people of every nation, language, and ethnic group. Many commentators translate this "universal" to distinguish it from the Catholic Church that is centered in the See of Rome. Such a distinction is difficult to justify as *katholikos* already begins to take on specific meaning in the second century. See the essay on the church in chapter 4.

16 Most scholars of early Christianity think that holding an agape feast (*poieo*

approves is pleasing to God so that everything that is practiced may be certain and valid.[17]

Chapter 9

(1) Finally, it is reasonable to become sober again and, as we have opportunity, to repent toward God. It is a good thing to recognize God and the bishop. The one who honors the bishop has been honored by God. The one who does something secretly from the bishop serves the devil. (2) For you, let everything abound in grace for you are worthy. You have refreshed me in every way and Jesus Christ has refreshed you. You have loved me whether I was absent or present. May God reward you for whose sake, if you endure all things, you will reach him.

Chapter 10

Now as for Philo and Rheus Agathopous who have followed me for the word of God, you have done well to receive them as deacons of Christ, of God. They give thanks to the Lord for you because you have refreshed them in every way. Nothing will be lost for you. (2) My spirit and my bonds are your substitute soul,[18] which things you need neither take pride in nor be ashamed of. Nor will the perfect faith,[19] that is Jesus Christ, ever make you ashamed.

---

agapen) was a large meal of which the celebration of the Eucharist was a part. Gradually these two parts were separated and the agape feast faded into disuse.

17 Ignatius gives us evidence that the validity of church practices was tied to apostolic succession in his mind. See chapter 4 on the church.

18 "substitute soul." For the theological significance of *antipsuchon* in Ignatius, see the essay on martyrdom in chapter 2.

19 Some MSS have "hope" which is the reading that Ehrman chose.

Chapter 11

(1) Your prayer has gone up for the church in Antioch of Syria. So, being bound with the most God-worthy fetters, I greet all although I am not worthy to be from there since I am the least. But I was counted worthy by [God's] will, not from conscience but from God's grace which I beg to be given in perfect measure that I may attain God by your prayers. (2) Therefore, that your work may be perfect on earth and in heaven, it is fitting that your church chose an ambassador for God's honor so that, having arrived in Syria, you may rejoice with them. This is because they will be at peace when they receive their own greatness, and their own corporate body[20] is restored. (3) It seemed to me a worthy matter to send someone of yours with a letter that it may celebrate the calm coming to them by God's design and since they already happened to find safe harbor by your prayer. Since you are perfect, set your mind on perfect things! God is ready to supply [what you need] for you who are willing to do good.

Chapter 12

(1) The love of the brothers in Troas greets you and so I write through Burrhus whom you sent with me together with the Ephesians, our brothers. He has refreshed me in every way. O that all would imitate him because he is a stellar example of a deacon of God! Grace will reward him in every way. (2) Now as for your worthy bishop, the God-honoring presbytery, and my fellow servants, the deacons, and in fact all who have human things in common, I greet them in the name of Jesus Christ, in his flesh and blood, in suffering and resurrection, in the unity

---

20 *somateion* ("corporate body"). This word occurs only here in the Ignatian corpus.

of God, both corporeal and spiritual. Grace to you, mercy, peace, patience continually.

Chapter 13

(1) I greet the homes of my brothers with their wives and children along with the virgins who are called widows. Farewell from me in the power of the Spirit.[21] Philo who is with me greets you. (2) I greet the house of Tavia which I wish to be established in faith and love bodily and spiritually. I greet Alce, a person very desired by me.[22] I also greet the incomparable Daphne and Eutecnus and all by name. Farewell in the grace of God.

---

21 Some MSS have "the Spirit of the Father" which is the reading Ehrman and others accept.

22 Lit. "a name desired by me," but name is often used as a synecdoche for the person as in the Bible.

Chapter Thirteen
Ignatius's Letter to Polycarp
Translation and Commentary

This shorter letter to Polycarp, the bishop of Smyrna, comple-
ments the longer letter to the church as a whole. Here Ignatius
urges his fellow bishop to be a faithful shepherd of the flock by
his personal holiness and careful watch over the church. The letter contains many characteristics similar to Paul's Pastoral
Epistles. Like Paul, Ignatius encourages forbearance (1:2), prayer
(1:3), concern for widows (4:1), and avoidance of evil practices
current in the Greco-Roman world (5:1). Chapters 1 to 5 use the
singular form of the pronoun "you" addressed to Polycarp, but
the rest of the letter employs the plural "you" addressed to the
whole church at Smyrna. Ancient letters were often expected to
be read by more than the explicit recipient. We know more about
Polycarp than any of the other bishops mentioned in these letters
(e.g. Damas, Polybius) because we have an account of his martyrdom as well as references in the writings of other early church
fathers (e.g. Irenaeus).

Salutation

Ignatius, called Theophorus, to the shepherd of the church of the Smyrneans, or rather to him who is shepherded by God the Father and the Lord Jesus Christ.[1] Hearty Greetings!

Chapter 1

(1) Upon receiving your will in God which is established as on an immovable rock, I highly magnify [God] since I was counted worthy [of seeing] your blameless face that I enjoy in God. (2) I encourage you in that grace with which you are clothed to set your course and encourage everyone to be saved. Vindicate your position with a physical and spiritual diligence. Pay attention to unity than which there is nothing better. Bear with all as the Lord has with you. Be forbearing in love as you already are doing. (3) Linger constantly in prayers.[2] Seek a greater understanding than you have. Be alert with that sleepless spirit you obtained. Speak to each one in union with God's moral character.[3] Bear the sicknesses of all as a perfect athlete. Where there is more labor, there is much gain.

---

1   Here I have translated *episkopos* (bishop) as "shepherd" to keep the parallel with the verb Ignatius uses (*episkopeo*), i.e. "him who is shepherded by God."

2   Ignatius's exhortation to pray constantly draws on Paul in 1 Thess 5:17. Both authors use *adialeiptos* ("unceasingly"). Ignatius uses a word not associated with prayer in the NT. *Scholaze* normally means "be at leisure." Thus my "linger" with respect to prayer. Holmes has "be devoted to." Ehrman has "be assiduous" while Camelot chooses *vaquer.*

3   *kata homoetheian theou* ("in unity with God"). This phrase can have several meanings. My translation is intimated by Camelot's "dans l'unité d'espirit avec Dieu." Ehrman has "according to God's own character."

Chapter 2

(1) If you love good disciples, it is no profit for you. Rather, in meekness bring those who are the more troublesome into subjection. Not every wound is healed with the same cure. Calm the contentious with infusions [of love].[4] (2) Be wise as a serpent in everything and always harmless as a dove.[5] This is the reason you are physical and spiritual[6] that you may gently handle the things as they appear before you.[7] Ask that the invisible things will be shown to you so that you will not lack anything and abound in every [spiritual] gift. (3) The opportunity calls you as the helmsmen [of a ship] seeks the winds and as one in a storm seeks a harbor, so that you may reach God. Be vigilant as God's athlete. The prize is incorruption and eternal life[8] of which you have already been persuaded. I and my bonds that you love are your substitute soul[9] in every way.

Chapter 3

(1) Let not those who seem worthy of trust and yet who promote false teachings disturb you. Stand firm like an anvil being beaten. What makes a great athlete is the fighting and then achieving victory. We must especially endure all things for

---

4   See Ehrman, Holmes, and Camelot for different translations.

5   Compare Mt 10:16.

6   Another instance of Ignatius's repeated phrase "fleshly and spiritual."

7   There are several possible translations here. I have followed the example of Ehrman ("deal gently with what is visible before you") and Holmes ("treat gently whatever appears before you").

8   *thema* ("prize") can also mean "a case proposed." Most translate it "prize" because of the athletic metaphor immediately preceding. The sentence could also be rendered "It is a matter of incorruption and eternal life."

9   *antipsuchon*, see Polyc 6:1 and Eph 21:1; Smyrn 10: 2. See also the discussion of this term in chapter 2 on Ignatius's theology of martyrdom and in chapter 4 on the holiness of the church.

God's sake that he may endure us. (2) Be more diligent where you are. Discern the opportunities. Wait for him who is above the opportunity, the one who is timeless, the invisible one who became visible for our sake, the one who cannot be touched, the one incapable of suffering who came to suffer for our sake, the one who bore patiently every manner of difficulty.[10]

Chapter 4

(1) Do not let widows be neglected. After the Lord, be their wise guide. Let nothing be done without your consent or do anything apart from God which in fact you are not doing. Be steadfast! (2) Let your gatherings be more frequent. Seek out[11] everyone by name. (3) Do not lord it over male or female slaves but neither let them be puffed up. Rather, let them serve for God's glory that they may obtain a better freedom from God. Let them not desire to be set free at the church's expense[12] that they may not be found to be slaves of desire.

Chapter 5

(1) Flee evil arts.[13] It would be better to make speeches about them. Exhort my sisters to love the Lord and to please

---

10 The pastoral care of a faithful bishop follows the example of Christ who left heavenly glory to come to the pains of this world. This thought is similar to Paul's in 2 Cor 8:9, "you know the grace of our Lord Jesus Christ, that, being rich, he became poor for our sake that we might be enriched by his poverty."

11 Or it could be "he [God] seeks everyone out by name." *Zetei* could be 3sg. indicative or 2sg. imperative.

12 Lightfoot translates this phrase "at public expense."

13 *kakotechnia* ("flee evil arts") usually refers to magical arts in the mystery religions in Polycarp's culture, but Ignatius may be using it simply to encourage the bishop of Smyrna to avoid crafty and deceptive methods of ministry. Paul has a similar statement about his own ministry in 2 Cor 4:2.

their husbands in flesh and spirit. Similarly, command my brothers in the name of Jesus Christ to love their wives as Christ does the church.[14] (2) If anyone can remain in purity for the honor of the Lord's flesh, let him remain so without boasting. If he should boast, he has perished, and if it is known beyond the bishop, he is corrupted. It is fitting that men and women who marry seek unity with the will of the bishop[15] that the marriage may be in accord with the Lord's will and not by lust. Let all be done to the honor of God.

Chapter 6

(1) Pay attention to the bishop that God may do the same to you. I am the substitute soul[16] for those who are subject to the bishop, presbyters, and deacons. With them may I have some part in God. Work with one another, compete together, run together, suffer together, rest together, and get up together as God's stewards, companions,[17] and servants. (2) Seek to please the one in whose army you serve. From him you receive your wages. Let none of you be found to be a deserter. Let your baptism remain your weapons. Your faith is your helmet. Love is

---

14 Paul in Eph 5:25.

15 Lit. "make unity with the will of the bishop." Ignatius is here urging that marriage between Christians should be brought under the authority of the church. Nothing like this requirement occurs explicitly in the NT but one can easily see how it developed out of the many passages on marriage in Jesus's teaching (e.g. Mt 19:1-9; Mk 10:1-12) and Paul's (e.g. 1 Cor 7:1-40; Eph 5:22-33). As the idea of the unity of the church grew in the consciousness of early Christians, it was only natural that the most important of human institutions would be at the heart of the church's pastoral care.

16 See the comment at Polyc 2:3 and the discussions of *antipsuchon* in chapters 2 and 4.

17 Lightfoot translates *paredoi* as "assessors" while Ehrman has "attendants" and Holmes "assistants."

your spear. Endurance is your full armor.[18] Your down payment
is your works so that you can receive back wages. Be patient with
one another as God is with you. May I benefit from you always.

Chapter 7

(1) Since the church in Antioch of Syria is at peace because
of your prayer, as was shown to me, I have become more cheer-
ful and free from worry in God,[19] if in fact I may obtain God
through suffering so that I may be found to be a disciple in
your resurrection. (2) O most blessed Polycarp, it is fitting to
lead the God-worthy council and to elect someone to be
found worthy of going to Syria and honoring your eager love
for the glory of God. He must be very loving and eager to be
called a messenger for God. (3) The Christian does not have
his own authority; he gives his time to God.[20] This is God's
and your work when you fulfill it. I believe by grace that you
are ready to do good agreeable to God. Knowing your inten-
sity for truth, I encourage you in a few letters.

Chapter 8

(1) So since I was not able to write all the churches because I
had to sail suddenly from Troas to Neapolis, as the will [of God]
ordered it, will you write to the churches before me, as one possessing the mind of God, so that they do the same? Some are able to

---

18 See Paul Eph 6:11-17.

19 *en amerimnia theou* ("free from worry in God"), lit. "in a lack of concern of God."
Ignatius appears to mean that peace in the Antiochean church coming from
God's presence gives a certain freedom of anxiety.

20 "Gives his time to God." Lightfoot's translation of *theo scholazei*. Ehrman reads
another sense of *scholazei*, i.e. "is diligent for God."

send someone on foot; others by letters with those sent by you that you might be honored in an eternal work, since you are worthy. (2) I greet all by name and the wife of Epitropos with all her house and children. I greet Attalus my beloved [friend]. I greet the one who is counted worthy of going to Syria. Grace will be with him always and with Polycarp who sends him. (3) I wish you farewell always in our God, Jesus Christ. In him you remain in union with God and the bishop. I greet Alce, a name beloved by me. Farewell in the Lord.

Chapter Fourteen
Polycarp's Letter to the Philippians
Translation and Commentary

Polycarp shows himself in the *Letter to the Philippians* to be a capable pastor of the whole church. Drawing on a wide range of scriptural texts, the bishop of Smyrna weaves together an extended exhortation pointing the Philippians to the central truths of the gospel. Like Paul before him, Polycarp encourages what is good among the Macedonian church (e.g. 2:2) and repeats the biblical call to care for widows, orphans, and the poor (ch. 6). At the same time Polycarp warns the Philippians of moral and doctrinal deviation. The greatest moral threat to the Christian is the love of money to which the presbyter Valens and his wife fell prey (ch.11). Doctrinal problems with Docetism still seem to linger since the time of Ignatius (ch.7). Throughout the letter Polycarp exhorts his readers to endurance in the face of suffering, perhaps aware that his own martyrdom may not be too distant.

Salutation

Polycarp and the presbyters with him [write] to the church of God on its journey at Philippi. May mercy and peace from God Almighty and from Jesus Christ our Savior be multiplied to you.

Chapter 1

(1) I rejoiced greatly in our Lord Jesus Christ with you who received the remembrances of true love[1] and who sent on those bound in the bonds fitted for saints, as it was incumbent on you.[2] These are the diadems of those truly chosen by God and our Lord.[3] (2) [I also rejoice] because the firm root of your faith, proclaimed from ancient times, remains even now, and is bearing fruit for our Lord Jesus Christ. He patiently endured for our sins even to the point of death. It was He that God raised from the dead having undone the pangs of hell.[4] (3) Even though you do not see him, you believe with an ineffable joy that is full of glory.[5] Many desire to enter this joy because they know that you have been saved by grace, not from works,[6] but rather by the will of God and through Jesus Christ.

---

1 *mimema* is translated variously as "representations" (Lightfoot, Holmes) or "replicas" (Ehrman). I have chosen "remembrances" because it seems to refer to some token of Polycarp's love sent with Ignatius.

2 Those sent on is probably a reference to Ignatius and his companions who traveled through Philippi on the way to Rome.

3 Seeing the chains of martyrdom as crowns of eternal life indicates how these early Christian leaders were imbued with a courage beyond human power.

4 See Acts 2:24. Polycarp here reflects Paul's theology on the centrality of the death and resurrection of Jesus (the Paschal Mystery) as the key to all salvation and life.

5 A quotation from 1 Pet 1:8 where the apostle speaks of the Christian having "an inexpressible and glorious joy."

6 "Saved by grace and not from works" is a quotation from Ephesians 2:5, 8-9.

Chapter 2

(1) So, girding your loins, serve[7] God in reverence and truth as you abandon the empty words and deception of the crowd placing your trust in the One who raised our Lord Jesus Christ from the dead and who gave him glory and a throne at His right hand. Everything in heaven and on earth is subject to Him. Every breathing thing serves[8] Him who is coming as judge of the living and of the dead. God will require his blood from those who disobey Him. (2) He who raised him (Jesus) from the dead will also raise us[9] if we do his will and walk in his commands and love the things he loved, abstaining from all injustice, greed, love of money, foul speech, and false witness, not returning evil for evil or abuse for abuse,[10] or blow for blow, or cursing for cursing. (3) We must remember what the Lord taught, "Do not judge that you may not be judged. Forgive and it will be forgiven you. Be merciful that you may receive mercy. The measure which you use to measure others is the same one by which you yourselves will be measured."[11] He also said, "Blessed are the poor and those persecuted for the sake of righteousness because theirs is the kingdom of God."[12]

Chapter 3

(1) Brothers, I do not write these things to you on my own initiative about this righteousness but because you requested it of me. (2) Neither I nor anyone like me is able to emulate the

---

7   Ehrman translates "serve as God's slaves" because Polycarp uses *douleuo*, a verb related to *doulos* meaning slave.

8   Polycarp here uses *latreuo* ("to serve"). In Christian Greek it can connote service of worship.

9   For a possible parallel see 2 Cor 4:14.

10   See 1 Pet 3:9.

11   Polycarp here quotes the words of Jesus as in Mt 7:1,2 and Lk 6:36-38.

12   See Lk 6:20 (and Mt 5:3?) and Mt 5:10.

wisdom of the blessed and glorious Paul who, when he came among you in person, taught the message of truth accurately and firmly. When absent, he wrote you letters[13] by which, if you studied closely, you can be built up further in the faith given you. (3) This faith is the mother of us all[14] as hope accompanies it with love leading the way to God, Christ, and neighbor.[15] If any one is centered on these, he has fulfilled the command of righteousness.[16] For the one who has love is far from all sin.

Chapter 4

(1) The love of money is the beginning of all hardships.[17] Knowing, therefore, that we brought nothing into the world,

---

13 Some scholars say that this reference to "letters" written by Paul to the Philippians is consistent with the hypothesis that Paul's letter in the NT is in fact a compilation of several letters to the church at Philippi and that Polycarp knew this. It is difficult to see Paul's Letter to the Philippians as a composite letter. Polycarp may have been thinking of Paul's letter bound with other NT letters and sent to the Philippians. This would also explain his use of the plural "letters."

14 See Gal 4:26 where Paul calls the heavenly Jerusalem "our mother." The account of the martyrdom of Justin in the second century also speaks of faith as our mother. Later Christian writers will apply the metaphor to the church. The term mother refers to heaven, the church, or to the faith because each has a part in imparting the new birth to the baptized (see Jn 3:3,5).

15 The triad of faith, hope, and love recalls Paul's words in 1 Cor 13:13.

16 The word "righteousness" is probably used here in the wider sense of justice, modeled on the Hebrew phrase *mishpat-tsedek* (requirement of justice) that had a strong social connotation in the OT. Here Polycarp says that true justice is the internal justice or rightness produced by faith, hope, and love and which produces justice in our external relations.

17 A paraphrase of Paul's words in 1 Tim 6:10. At first glance it is not clear why love of money as opposed to some other kind of sin should be the root of all evil or hardship. But Polycarp, following Paul, may be using love of money as a synecdoche, i.e. a particular example of a larger principle. Attachment to things of this life runs counter to the desire for eternal life. The desire for union with God via martyrdom purifies the soul of earthly attachments to liberate it from what must be relinquished in the end.

and have nothing to take with us out of it,[18] let us fight with the weapons of righteousness and let us teach ourselves first of all to walk in the Lord's command. (2) Then also your wives [should remain] in the faith, love, and purity given to them by being affectionate toward their own husbands in all truth, and loving all equally with all self-control[19] and to teach their children the instruction [coming from] reverence for God. (3) Widows too should be prudent about faith in the Lord,[20] interceding constantly for all. [They should stay] far away from all slander, evil speech, false witness, love of money, and all evil. [They should] know that they are God's altar and everything is inspected for defects.[21] Nothing escapes his notice, not thoughts, not intentions, not anything else hidden in the heart.[22]

Chapter 5

(1) Since we know that God is not mocked, we ought to walk worthily of his command and his glory. (2) Similarly, deacons ought to be blameless in the presence of his righteousness as they are servants[23] of God and of Christ and not of men. They

---

18 A paraphrase of Paul's words in 1 Tim 6:7.

19 "Self-control" or "self-restraint" (Ehrman) is to be preferred to "chastity" (Lightfoot, Holmes) as *egkrateia* is not limited to sexual desire.

20 *sophroneo* ("prudent") is translated by Holmes as "think soberly" and by Ehrman "self-controlled." *Sophroneo* in Christian Geek is a wide-ranging virtue of temperance or prudence, meaning self-restraint in food, drink, and desire.

21 *momoskopeitai* ("inspected for defects") a word used for inspecting defects in a sacrificial offering. Polycarp here honors the widows of the church by calling them God's altar. Their lives are as precious to God as any offering on an altar but they must take care lest their lives are marred by sin. His views are clearly dependent on Paul (see 1 Tim 5:3-16; Tit 2:3,4) who in turn depended on the OT prescriptions on caring for the widow and orphan (see e.g. Ps 146:9).

22 Polycarp here reflects the same sentiment of Heb 4:13, "There is not one creature who is not apparent to him."

23 *diakonos* is translated "deacon" in the first instance to designate the title of the office while "servant" in the second to designate the primary function of the office.

should not be slanderers or deceptive; they should be free from the love of money, self-controlled in everything, compassionate, caring, living in accord with the Lord's truth who became a servant of all. If we are pleasing to Him in the present age, we will receive the future age as he has reserved for us rising from the dead. If we conduct ourselves worthily[24] of him, we will reign[25] with him if indeed we believe. (3) Likewise, younger men should be blameless in every respect, putting purity above everything and steering themselves away from every evil. It is good to restrain ourselves from the evil desires in the world because every evil desire wars against the spirit[26] and neither immoral people, nor effeminate,[27] nor homosexuals will inherit the kingdom of God, not even those who practice aberrant forms of behavior. Therefore, it is necessary that those who are subject to the presbyters and deacons as to God and Christ abstain from all these things and that the virgins walk in a blameless and pure conscience.

Chapter 6

(1) Let the presbyters be compassionate, merciful to all, converting those who are deceived, carefully watching over all the weak, not neglecting widows, or orphans, or the poor. Rather, plan ahead for what is beautiful in the sight of God and man, abstaining from all anger, discrimination against persons,[28]

---

24 *politeuomai* connotes personal conduct in reference to one's contemporary society.

25 For a similar promise of reigning with Christ see in 1 Tim 2:12. See also Rom 8:17.

26 "Spirit" could refer to the human spirit or the Spirit of God.

27 *pornoi* ("immoral people") refers to the sexually immoral. "Effeminate" translates *malakoi* which generally means soft or even cowardly. Polycarp may here be using it to speak of those who are morally weak (1 Cor 6:9).

28 The traditional translation for *prosopolempsia* is "respect of persons," but is clearly used to mean unjust discrimination based on social status. See Jas 2:1.

unjust judgment, remaining far from the love of money. Do not
believe something against anyone too quickly; don't be severe
in judgment because you know that we are all subject to sin.[29]
(2) So, if we beg the Lord that he forgive us, we too ought to
forgive. For we live in the sight of (our) Lord and God, and it is
necessary that we all stand before the judgment seat of Christ[30]
and that each give an account of himself. (3) So in this manner
let us serve him with reverence and all piety just as he (Christ),
along with the apostles and prophets who preached, commanded us. They proclaimed to us the coming of our Lord
ahead of time. They[31] were zealous for the good, abstaining
from the scandals of false brethren and those who carry the
name of the Lord in hypocrisy. Such men deceive empty-head-
ed people.

Chapter 7

(1) Everyone who does not confess that Jesus Christ has
come in the flesh is an antichrist.[32] And whoever does not confess the witness of the cross is of the devil.[33] Whoever distorts
the sayings of the Lord for his own desires and claims that there
is neither a resurrection nor a judgment, is the firstborn of

29 "Subject to sin," i.e. liable to fall into sin. We should not be judgmental toward
others because we ourselves can easily fall into sin. Ehrman's translation ("in
debt because of sin") gives it a slightly different meaning.

30 Polycarp seems to be conflating Rom 14:10 with 2 Cor 5:10 since both refer to
the judgment seat (*bema*) of Christ.

31 Most scholars (e.g. Camelot, Ehrman) translate this "we should be zealous" (i.e.
an exhortation). That certainly fits the context but the most natural grammatical
connection implies that Polycarp is speaking about the exemplary behavior of
apostles.

32 Polycarp quotes from 1 Jn 4:2,3.

33 The phrase "of the devil" seems to be taken from 1 Jn 3:8 which says, "The one
who practices sin is of the devil."

Satan.[34] (2) So, abandoning the futility of the crowd and false teachings, let us return to the message handed down to us from the beginning as we are alert in prayer and persevering in fasting, making our request of the all-seeing God that he lead us not into temptation.[35] It is as the Lord said, "the spirit is willing but the flesh is weak."[36]

Chapter 8

(1) Let us unceasingly cling to our hope and to the down payment on our righteousness,[37] who is Christ Jesus. He is the one "who bore our sins in his own body on the tree, who did no sin, nor was any guile found in his mouth."[38] But he endured all things that we might live in him. (2) Let us become imitators of his endurance. If we suffer on behalf of his name, we should give him the glory. Through his own example, he gave us a model and we ourselves have put our trust in this.

Chapter 9

(1) So, I appeal to you to obey the word of righteousness and to endure with all endurance. You know this endurance

---

34 In the Moscow manuscript version of the *Martyrdom of Polycarp* (chapter 22), Polycarp calls Marcion "the firstborn of Satan."

35 See Mt 6:13.

36 Mt 26:41. In chapter 7, Polycarp here teaches that there are two ways to deviate from the path of Christ. One is outright denial, i.e. to deny that Christ has come in the flesh or that he died on the cross for our sins. The second deviation is to interpret the words of Christ according to one's own preconceived ideas, i.e. "to distort the sayings of the Lord." The latter has proven to be the more common in the history of Christianity.

37 "Down payment" is the word *arrabon*. This word used by Paul of the Holy Spirit in Eph 1:14. Polycarp may be thinking of baptism as the foundation of future life. In baptism the righteousness conferred acts as a down payment of future glory.

38 1 Pet 2:24,22.

personally,[39] not only in the blessed Ignatius, Zosimus, and Rufus but also in others from your number and in Paul himself and in the other apostles. (2) You are persuaded that all these did not run in vain but in faith and righteousness, and that they are with the Lord with whom they suffered in that place owed them.[40] They did not love the present age[41] but him who died for us and was raised again by God for our sakes.

Chapter 10[42]

(1) So, stand in these things and follow the example of the Lord, firm and immovable in faith, lovers of the brotherhood,[43] loving one another, bound together in truth, waiting on one another in the gentleness of the Lord, despising no one.[44] (2) When you are able to do good, do not put it off because "alms liberate from death."[45] Let all be subject to one another, holding the ways of your life above reproach among the Gentiles that you may receive praise because of your good works and the Lord may not be blasphemed among you. (3) But "woe to him through whom the name of the Lord is blasphemed."[46] So teach all to be sober as you yourselves are doing.

---

39 *kat' ophthalmous* ("personally"), lit. "with your own eyes" (Ehrman).

40 Polycarp here shows his dependence on Paul's thinking when he speaks of suffering with Christ. Paul writes of this often. See Rom 6:8; 8:17; 2 Cor 1:5; Col 1:24; 2 Tim 2:12.

41 In 2 Tim 4:10 Paul speaks of Demas "who loved the present age." For both Paul and Polycarp, attachment to this world endangers one's prospects for inheriting eternal glory because it means loving the creature instead of "him who died and rose again."

42 Chapters 10, 11, 12 and 14 survive only in Latin translation.

43 See 1 Pet 2:17 for Peter's exhortation to love the brotherhood.

44 All the phrases in this first section of chapter 10 echo the exhortations of Paul in his letters. See e.g. Rom 12:9-13.

45 Tobit 4:10 or 12:9.

46 Is 52:5.

Chapter 11

(1) I am very grieved about Valens, who was once made a presbyter among you, because he so misunderstands the position given to him. So I warn you to abstain from love of money and be pure and truthful. Abstain from every [kind of] of evil. (2) Whoever cannot govern himself, how can he preach to others? If anyone fails to abstain from love of money, he will be defiled by idolatry and will be judged like one among the Gentiles who know nothing of the judgment of the Lord. Do we not know that "the saints will judge the world," as Paul said?[47] (3) But I have neither perceived nor heard of anything like this among you, among whom blessed[48] Paul labored, you who are [addressed] in the beginning of his letter. He gloried in you among all the churches that alone knew God at that time. We had not yet come to know [him]. (4) So, brothers, I am sad about him (Valens) and his wife. May the Lord give them true repentance! You too must be sober in this matter and not think of such people as enemies, but rather call them back as suffering and erring members that your entire body may be saved. By doing this you will be built up.

Chapter 12

(1) I am confident that you are well versed in the sacred writings and nothing is hidden from you; to me this has not been granted.[49] Only, as it is said in the Scriptures, "Be angry and do not sin" and "do not let the sun go down on your

---

47 1 Cor 6:2.

48 "Blessed" is the beginning of the early Christian usage of this term as a title.

49 This statement about Polycarp not understanding the Scriptures seems strange in the light of (1) his being a teacher (bishop) of the church and (2) his obvious use of the Bible. The best explanation offered by many scholars (e.g. Berding) is that Polycarp is here displaying humility, either genuinely or in a slightly affected manner.

anger."[50] Blessed is the one who remembers this. I believe such is the case among you. (2) However, may the God and Father of our Lord Jesus Christ, and the eternal priest himself Jesus Christ, build you up in faith, truth, and all gentleness without anger, in endurance, in long-suffering, tolerance, and purity. May God grant you a portion and an inheritance among his saints — to us and you as well. And may he give to all who are under heaven, who will believe in our Lord and God, Jesus Christ, and in his Father who raised him from the dead. (3) Pray for all God's holy ones. Pray also for kings, magistrates, and rulers, and for all who persecute and hate you and are enemies of the cross, that your fruit may be evident in all, that you may be perfect in him.[51]

Chapter 13

(1) You and Ignatius wrote to me that if anyone departs for Syria, he should carry along the letters from you. I myself will do this if I have a suitable opportunity, or [send] someone who is an ambassador for you. (2) The letters of Ignatius sent by him to you and the others that we had with us, we sent to you as you commanded. These latter are appended to this letter. From these you can receive great profit. They contain faith, endurance, and everything that edifies, things fitting for our Lord.

---

50 Eph 4:26 where Paul quotes Ps 4:5.

51 This section of chapter 12 is Polycarp's application of Mt 5:43-48 where God's loving care even for his enemies is enjoined as the reason why Christians should love their enemies and pray for their persecutors. Being perfect as the heavenly Father is, requires going beyond the normal human expectation of treating others as we are treated. It requires loving even those who hate us.

Chapter 14

(1) I wrote you these things through Crescens whom I have commended when present and whom I now commend. His behavior has been blameless. I believe that he will be the same among you as well. His sister too will be commended to you when she arrives. Be safe in the Lord Jesus Christ in grace with all yours. Amen.

Chapter Fifteen
The Martyrdom of Polycarp
Translation and Commentary

The *Martyrdom of Polycarp* is one of the earliest and fullest accounts of an early Christian martyr that we possess. The author, probably writing not long after Polycarp's death, distinguishes between true and false martyrdom (ch 3, 4). Martyrdom "according to the gospel" is not a voluntary offering of oneself but a willingness to accept death in imitation of Christ. Chapter two is an initial explanation of true martyrdom from which he then proceeds to recount how Polycarp was a model of Christlike endurance. This treatise shows how early the intercession of the Saints occurred in the church (17:3) and how early Christians desired to honor the remains of their martyrs.

Salutation

The church of God sojourning at Smyrna to the church of God sojourning at Philomelium and to all those sojourners of the holy and catholic church in every place.[1] May the mercy, peace, and love of God the Father and the Lord Jesus Christ be multiplied.

Chapter 1

(1) We wrote to you, brothers, those things about those who had given testimony[2] and blessed Polycarp. Having sealed it with his martyrdom, he caused the persecution to cease. Almost all these proceedings happened that the Lord may show us again[3] [the meaning of] martyrdom according to the gospel[4] (2) He waited patiently to be delivered up, as the Lord [was] for us, to become his imitators, by looking out not only for ourselves but also for our neighbor. It is a matter of true and firm love to wish for salvation not only for ourselves but for all the brethren.[5]

---

1   The term "sojourning" is used in Christian literature in contrast to heaven that is the homeland (*patria*) of the faithful. The NT writers use it extensively. See Eph 2:19; 1 Pet 2:11 and especially Heb 11:9,10 where Abraham is the premier example of sojourning. Polycarp uses the word in Phil Polyc Sal. For more on the use of "catholic" see chapter four in the introductory essays.

2   This could also be translated "those who suffered martyrdom."

3   *anothen* ("again") could be translated "from above" in which case the author means that God is watching over the martyrdom to use it as way of forming Christians in the gospel.

4   Martyrdom according to the gospel represents in a phrase the core of why this martyrdom was written down.

5   The author here explains the meaning of martyrdom according to the gospel. It is an act of love for others to show them the way of obedience to God even if it involves one's death.

Chapter 2

(1) Blessed and noble indeed are all the martyrdoms which have happened according to the will of God. For we should be even more pious so as to attribute to God authority over all things. (2) For who could fail to be amazed at their noble character, their endurance, and their love of the Master? They endured when lacerated with whips to the point that their flesh showed down to their arteries and veins, as the onlookers moaned with compassion. But not one of those who achieved so great a nobility groaned or moaned, showing us all that in that very hour Christ's witnesses vacated their flesh under torture because the Lord was there conversing with them. (3) Clinging to the grace of Christ, they despised worldly torments as they were redeemed from eternal punishment in just one hour. For them, the fire of their human tormentors was cold for they had before their eyes the thought of escaping the eternal [fire] that is never extinguished. And with the eyes of the heart they gazed upward to the good things reserved for those who endure, things that "neither ear has heard, nor eye has seen, nor have even arisen in the human heart."[6] These things were shown by the Lord to them who were no longer men but already angels. (4) Likewise, those who were condemned to the beasts endured horrible punishments, being stretched out on sharp shells and punished with various kinds of torments. The tyrant did this so that, if possible, he could bring them to denial through this long lasting punishment.

Chapter 3

(1) The devil devised many things against them,[7] but

---

6   1 Cor 2:9.

7   This first sentence of 3:1 occurs at the end of chapter 2 in some editions. See Holmes p. 308.

thanks be to God, he could not prevail against them. The most noble Germanicus emboldened their cowardice with the endurance in him who battled the beasts in a remarkable way. Although the proconsul[8] wanted to persuade him by saying that he should have compassion on his age, Germanicus drew the beast to himself wanting quickly to exchange their unjust and lawless life.[9] (2) So, from this, the whole crowd, amazed at the noble character of the God-loving and God-worshiping tribe of Christians cried out, "Take away those who deny the gods."[10] Let Polycarp be sought."

Chapter 4

(1) There was one man by the name of Quintus, a Phrygian, recently arrived from Phrygia, who cowered when he saw the beasts. This man urged himself and others to come forward willingly. The proconsul, when he had entreated him earnestly many times, persuaded him to swear an oath and to sacrifice.[11] For this reason, brothers, we do not praise those who deliver themselves over since the gospel does not teach this.[12]

---

8   The author names the proconsul Statius Quadratus in chapter 21. A man by this name was known to be the proconsul of Asia in A.D. 142 and may be the same person mentioned here. Our author portrays him as one who was reluctant to put the Christians to death. See chapters 4, 9, and 10.

9   I.e. exchange this ordinary life (*bios*) for eternal life that martyrdom would afford.

10 *atheous* ("those who deny the gods") lit. "atheists." The words of the crowd may mean that they did not want the entire group of Christians to be punished but only to silence them by doing away with their leader on the assumption that if the shepherd is struck down, the sheep will scatter. Or, as Lightfoot takes it, it may mean execution.

11 I.e. to the emperor and thus to the Roman gods.

12 See the discussion of false martyrdom in chapter six in the introductory essays.

Chapter 5

(1) At first, when he heard this, this most marvelous Polycarp was not disturbed but wanted to stay in the city. But the majority persuaded him to leave. He left for the country not far from the city and stayed there a little while. Night and day he did nothing else than pray for everyone and for the churches spread throughout the world. This was already his custom.[13] (2) While praying, he [Polycarp] had a vision that before three days he would be arrested and he saw his pillow being burned up by fire.[14] Then he turned and said to his companions, "It is necessary that I be burned alive."

Chapter 6

(1) While those looking for him persisted in their search, he moved to [another part of the] countryside but when they arrived and did not find him, they seized two young slaves one of whom confessed under torture. (2) It was impossible for him to escape since those who betrayed him were of his family. And the magistrate who was called by the same name, Herod, hurried to bring him into the stadium that he may prepare for his own lot, having become a partaker of Christ.[15] But those who betrayed him made him suffer the punishment of Judas himself.[16]

---

13 An example of Polycarp's exhortations to prayer can be found in Phil Polyc chap.12.

14 This sentence could mean that he had the vision three days before being arrested. Ehrman and Holmes translate it so. I have taken "before three days" to be in the infinitival clause and therefore as part of the vision.

15 Some translations assume that Polycarp's becoming a partaker of Christ was Herod's intention, in which case it probably means sharing in the same kind of death. On the other hand, being a sharer in Christ could be the writer's view that by martyrdom Polycarp would come to share in Christ in a deeper mystical sense.

16 Throughout subsequent Christian history, Judas becomes the archetype of betrayal.

Chapter 7

(1) Since the persecutors and the horsemen held the small boy on Friday[17] around the dinner hour, they left with their customary weapons as if running after a thief. At a later hour, when they converged, they found him (Polycarp) sitting in a certain upper bedroom. Now from there he was able to escape to another place but he did not wish to. He said, "let the will of God be done." (2) When he heard them coming, he went down and conversed with them. They were amazed at his age and composure and wondered whether there was [a need for] such eagerness to arrest such an old man. At once he ordered them to sit down, and to eat and drink as much as they wanted for an hour. He begged them to give him an hour to pray undisturbed. (3) Since they permitted him, he faced the east[18] and prayed since he was full of God's grace in this way. He was unable to be silent for two hours and he drove all his hearers to repent for having come for such a God-fearing old man.

Chapter 8

(1) At that time Polycarp finished his prayer after remembering all whom he had ever encountered: great and small, inglorious and glorious, as well as the whole catholic church throughout the known world. Once the hour had come to depart, they sat him on a donkey and they led him into the city on the great Sabbath.[19] (2) The magistrate Herod and his

---

17 *paraskeue* ("Friday") lit "the day of preparation." Early Gentile Christians adopted the Jewish names for days of the week.

18 One manuscript has the words "the east" which Murusillo adopts. Early Christians usually prayed facing the east since all prayer was directed to the risen Christ, symbolized by the sun rising. The eastern churches still pray their liturgies facing the east today.

19 There can be little doubt that the author wanted to draw the parallel between Polycarp's entry into Smyrna and Jesus's entry into Jerusalem (see Mt 21:1-11

father Nicetas met him. When they transferred him to a carriage, they sat beside him and said, "What harm is there in saying that Caesar is Lord and to make the required sacrifice and be saved?" At first he said nothing to them but while they stayed there, he said, "I am not going to do what you advise." (3) Those who failed to persuade him kept saying such horrible words and they hastily they seized him to drag him from the carriage as he bruised his shin. Not turning back as if he had no injury, he was willingly led to the stadium where there was such a great disturbance in the stadium that no one could hear anything.

Chapter 9

(1) A voice came from heaven to Polycarp as he entered the stadium, "Be strong, Polycarp, and play the man."[20] No one saw the one who spoke but those of us present heard the voice. And finally, after he was brought forward, there was a great disturbance among those who heard that Polycarp had been arrested. (2) The proconsul asked the man who had been brought forward, if he was Polycarp. When he admitted it, the proconsul kept trying to persuade him to deny it with these words, "Have respect for your age" and other words like these, as was their custom. "Swear by the good fortune of Caesar. Change your mind. Say away with the atheists." But Polycarp

---

and parallels). Calling the day "a great Sabbath" (cf. Jn 19:31) implicitly likens the bishop's death to Jesus's on the cross. This linkage between the two deaths suggests that for the author, Polycarp's death was more than an example of courage. Polycarp participated in the saving mission of Jesus by giving his own life for the church.

20 *andrizou* ("play the man"); a more literal translation than Holmes's "be courageous." This expression, which endured in English literature into the nineteenth century, has fallen into disuse. It reflects the classic idea that courage is a manly virtue.

looked sternly at the whole crowd of lawless Gentiles in the stadium. When he looked up and waved his hand, he sighed, lifted his eyes to heaven saying, "Away with the atheists." (3) As the proconsul was insistent, he said, "Swear and I will release you. Revile Christ!" But Polycarp said, "I have served him eight-six years and he has done me no wrong. How can I blaspheme my King who saved me?"

Chapter 10

(1) Again, the proconsul continued to urge him, "Swear by the good fortune of Caesar!" Polycarp answered, "if you imagine that I will swear by the good fortune of Caesar, as you say, you must be pretending to be ignorant of who I am. Listen with assurance! I am a Christian. If you wish to learn the teaching of Christianity, set a day and I will explain.[21] The proconsul said, "Persuade the people." (2) But Polycarp said, "I have counted you worthy for we have been taught to show fitting honor to the powers and authorities ordered by God. But I do not consider those [crowds] worthy of [hearing] a defense.[22]

Chapter 11

(1) The proconsul said, "I have beasts here. I will toss you to them if you do not change your mind. But he [Polycarp] said, "Call them. Change from the better to the worse is an impossible change for us. It is good to change from hard things to just things." (2) Again he [the proconsul] said to him, "I will have you destroyed by fire if you despise the beasts, if you do not

---

21 *akouson* ("I will explain"), lit "listen." This was a common manner of speech in ancient Greek but modern people express the same thought as translated above.

22 It is not clear why Polycarp did not consider the crowds worthy of hearing the message of Christianity but it does remind one of Jesus's words in Mt 7:6, "Don't cast your pearls before swine."

change your mind." But Polycarp said, "You threaten with the fire that burns for a time (hour) and after a little while is snuffed out. You are ignorant of the fire of the coming judgment and of eternal punishment that is reserved for the ungodly. But why do you hesitate? Bring on whatever you want."

Chapter 12

(1) When Polycarp said these and many more things, he was filled with courage and joy and his face was filled with grace[23] so that not only did the terrible things said by them not happen,[24] but, on the contrary, the proconsul stood in amazement. He sent his messenger into the middle of the stadium to announce three times, "Polycarp has confessed to being a Christian." (2) When the messenger said this, the whole crowd of gentiles, Jews, and the residents of Smyrna cried out in a loud voice with an uncontrollable rage, "This is the teacher of Asia, the father of Christians, the destroyer of our gods, the one who teaches many not to sacrifice or worship." When they had said these things, they cried out and begged the Asiarch Philip to let a lion loose on Polycarp. But he said that it was not legal since the hunting season was over.[25] (3) Then they seemed to cry out with one accord that Polycarp be burned alive. For the vision that had appeared to him on his pillow had to be fulfilled when he saw [the fire] burning as he prayed, he turned to the faithful

---

23 Polycarp's joy in the midst of suffering and impending death will be repeated many times in the history of Christian martyrdom. There are often extraordinary supernatural graces experienced by those whom God calls to martyrdom.

24 This sentence could be translated several different ways. See Ehrman and Holmes for alternatives.

25 The proconsul and Philip the Asiarch wanted to forgo responsibility by letting the crowd decide Polycarp's fate. This has significant parallels with the portrayal of Pontius Pilate in Jesus's death.

with him and spoke prophetically, "I must be burned alive."[26]

Chapter 13

(1) These things happened with greater speed than was said. Immediately, the crowds gathered wood and firewood from the workshops and the baths — especially the Jews helped, as was their custom. (2) When the fire was prepared, Polycarp took off his garments and, loosening his belt, he tried to untie his sandals. He had not previously done this because all of the faithful were anxious to touch his skin. In every respect, he was adorned on account of his good citizenship[27] and before his martyrdom. (3) At once then the instruments prepared for the fire were placed around him. As they were about to nail him, he said, "Leave me alone. He who gave me what I needed to endure the fire will also give me the ability to remain here unmoved without the security of your nails."

Chapter 14

(1) They did not nail him but rather bound him. They tied his hands behind his back and bound him like a singular ram from a big flock like a holocaust, made acceptable to God. When he gazed up to heaven he [Polycarp] said, "Lord God Almighty, father of your beloved and blessed child Jesus Christ. Through him we have received knowledge of you, the God of angels and powers and of all creation and of the race of the righteous who live before you. (2) I bless you because you have thought me worthy of this day and this hour to be numbered

---

26 Polycarp's joy and courage arose from his acceptance of his destiny as being from the hand of God.

27 *politeia* ("good citizenship"). I have chosen to retain the social meaning implied in *politeia* while Ehrman translates it "exemplary life" and Holmes "holy life."

among your martyrs in the cup of your Christ,[28] for the resurrection of eternal life, of both soul and body, in the incorruptibility of the Holy Spirit. Among these may I be received today before you, in the sacrifice that is rich and acceptable since you, the real and truthful God, have prepared, manifested, and fulfilled it.[29] (3) For this reason, I praise you for all things; I bless you; I glorify you through the eternal and heavenly high priest Jesus Christ your child. Through him and with him in the Holy Spirit be glory to you now and forevermore. Amen."[30]

Chapter 15

(1) When he had offered up the Amen and the prayer was finished, the men attending the fire lit it. As a great flame shot up we, to whom it was given to see, looked on this great wonder. We also were spared so that we may declare to others what happened. (2) The fire, making the form of an arch like a sail of a ship filled with the wind, formed a wall around the body of the martyr. And in the middle it was not like flesh burning but like bread baking or like gold and silver burning in an oven. For we perceived a sweet odor that was so strong that it was like frankincense wafting out or like some other precious aroma.[31]

---

28 "The cup of Christ" evokes Jesus's words in Mk 10:38 about the cup of suffering.

29 The sacrifice that Polycarp speaks of may be his own life or it may refer to the sacrifice of Christ in which he participates through his martyrdom. Ehrman and Holmes choose the former possibility and translate the phrase "as a rich and acceptable sacrifice." My translation is more literal by retaining the word "in." Even with a more literal version, however, the word *thusia* can be translated "a sacrifice" as well as "the sacrifice."

30 For an explanation of this prayer see chapter 6 in the introductory essays.

31 Perhaps this is part of the origin of "odor of sanctity" known in the history of Christian piety.

Chapter 16

(1) At last, when the lawless ones observed that his body could not be destroyed by fire, they commanded that the executioner be brought to stab him with a dagger. When he did this, a gush of blood[32] flowed out so that it extinguished the fire. The whole crowd was amazed that there was such a difference between the unbelievers and the elect. (2) One of these was this most astounding Polycarp who during our times became the bishop of the catholic church in Smyrna, an apostolic and prophetic teacher. Every word that left his mouth was fulfilled and would be fulfilled.

Chapter 17

(1) When he who is envious, jealous, and evil [the Devil], who opposes the righteous, saw the greatness of his [Polycarp's] martyrdom and his irreproachable conduct from the beginning, and [when he saw] him crowned with an incorruptible crown and rewarded with an indisputable prize, he tried to prevent us from removing his body although many desired to do this and to have fellowship with his holy flesh.[33] (2) He [the Evil One] incited Nicetas, Herod's father, Alce's brother, to entreat the ruler not to give the body [to the Christians] "lest," he said, "they leave the one crucified and they begin to worship this one. And the Jews incited and try to prevail in this way. They

---

32 Some MSS insert the words "dove and" so that Ehrman translates "a dove come forth along with such a quantity of blood." The editor of the text I am following omitted these words on the principle of adopting the shorter reading.

33 *koinonesai to agio autou sarkio* ("share in his holy flesh"). This is Ehrman's translation although he also notes that it could be rendered "commune with" or "have fellowship with." All of these are possible translations of *koinonesai*. Holmes's "touch his holy flesh" is too weak. Camelot rightly notes that we have here a very early (first?) expression of the cult of the martyrs. These Christians realized that prayer through the martyr's intercession was a way of sharing in the holiness of God from whom the martyr received the grace to suffer for Christ.

guarded us who were about to take him from the fire because they did not understand that we cannot abandon Christ who suffered blamelessly for sinners in the world who are being saved. Nor can we worship any other. (3) We worship him as the Son of God but we appropriately love the martyrs as disciples and imitators of the Lord on account of their unsurpassable affection for their king and teacher. May we become fellow partakers and disciples![34]

Chapter 18

(1) So, when the centurion saw the contentiousness of the Jews, he put [Polycarp] right in the middle and burned him as was their custom. (2) So we finally took his bones that were more precious than fine jewels and more refined than gold. We put them in a suitable place. (3) Then the Lord granted us who gathered in gladness and joy, as much as possible, to celebrate the birthday of his martyrdom for the memory of those who engaged the battle before us, and for the discipline and preparation of those who would follow.[35]

---

34 This wish explains the desire of the Christians to have Polycarp's body. The communion of Saints means that Christians on earth (church militant) and the inhabitants of heaven (church triumphant) share in the same graces bestowed on the martyr. By partaking in the same life and imitating the martyr Polycarp, the faithful of Smyrna will share the eternal glory Polycarp obtained by his death.

35 This sentence gives us insight into the beliefs of second-century Christians who were already celebrating feast days of the Saints or at least of the martyrs. Later in the century Tertullian of Carthage will speak of "offerings for the dead which we make on the anniversary of their birth" (i.e. to eternal life), Tertullian *On the Crown* ch. 3. Two reasons for the celebration of martyrs are given here in our text: (1) to remember their endurance and (2) to train those on earth who still engage the good fight (cf. 2 Tim 4:7) to follow the example of the martyrs' courage. For these early Christians the communion of the saints was very real.

Chapter 19

(1) Such are the things that happened to blessed Polycarp who was the twelfth to be martyred in Smyrna with those from Philadelphia. He alone is remembered by all so much so that he is mentioned by all the Gentiles everywhere. Not only was he a distinguished teacher but also an eminent witness. All longed to imitate his martyrdom in accord with the gospel of Christ. (2) Through endurance he prevailed over the unjust ruler and so obtained the incorruptible crown. Rejoicing with the apostles and all the righteous he glorifies the God and Father Almighty and blesses our Lord Jesus Christ, the Savior of our souls and the guide[36] of our bodies and Shepherd of the catholic church in the whole world.

Chapter 20

(1) You have deemed it valuable to be shown these events more fully but at the moment we have made them known only in summary through our brother Marcion.[37] Once you have learned these things, forward the letter to the brothers beyond, that they may glorify the Lord who makes choices from among his own servants.[38] (2) To Him who is able to lead us all in his grace and provides for [us to be in] his eternal kingdom through his child,[39] the only begotten Jesus Christ. To him may there be glory, honor, power, and majesty forever. Greet all the holy ones. Those with us greet you, as does Evaristus who wrote the letter, with his whole household.

---

36 *kubernetes* (guide) means the helmsman or captain of a ship.

37 Not to be confused with the famous heretic Marcion of the late second century.

38 God makes choice of martyrs through his providence. This hearkens back to chapter 4 where offering oneself for martyrdom, as Quintus the Phrygian did, was not noble. Only God chooses who will be martyred.

39 *pais* ("child") plays an important role in Polycarp's prayer in chapter 14. See also chapter six of my introductory essays for further discussion.

Chapter 21

(1) The blessed Polycarp gave this witness[40] on the second day of the month of Xanthikos, but among the Romans it is called seven days before the calends of March on the great Sabbath at the eighth hour.[41] He was arrested by Herod during the high priesthood Philip of Tralles while Statius Quadratus was proconsul but, more importantly, while Jesus Christ our Lord rules for ever.

Chapter 22 (version one)

(1) We bid you farewell, brothers, as you live in accord with the message of Jesus Christ in the gospel. To him be the glory with God the Father and the Holy Spirit for the salvation of his holy elect, just as blessed Polycarp gave witness.[42] May it be that we be found to walk in his footsteps in the kingdom of Jesus Christ. (2) Gaius transcribed this story from papers of Irenaeus, a disciple of Polycarp. Gaius lived together with Irenaeus in the same city. I, Socrates, wrote this in Corinth from the copies made by Gaius. Grace be with all! (3) Again, I, Pionius, wrote this down after seeking it out in accord with the revelation that blessed Polycarp showed me, as I will show in what follows. I gathered them together when they were nearly worn out from age, so that the Lord Jesus Christ may gather me too with his elect into his heavenly kingdom. To him be glory with the Father and the Holy Spirit forever and ever. Amen.

Chapter 22 (according to the Moscow manuscript)

(1) Gaius transcribed this story from the papers of

---

40 *marturei* (gave them witness) or "was martyred."

41 I.e. February 23 at 2:00 PM. The author no doubt added this detail to underscore the similarity between Polycarp's martyrdom and the death of Jesus.

42 *emarturesen* ("gave witness") or "was martyred."

Irenaeus. He lived with Irenaeus in the same city who was a disciple of holy Polycarp. (2) This Irenaeus was in Rome teaching many at the time of the martyrdom of bishop Polycarp. His many writings — both beautiful and correct — are still in circulation. In these he mentions Polycarp since he had been his pupil. He competently refuted every heresy and handed on the ecclesiastical and universal rule [of faith] that he had received from the Saint. (3) He [Irenaeus] told this story. When Marcion, from whom the Marcionites are named, once met Polycarp, he said to him, "You recognize us, Polycarp!" Then Polycarp responded, "I do recognize you! I recognize you as the firstborn of Satan!"[43] (4) And this was told in the writings of Irenaeus. On the day and the hour when Polycarp was martyred in Smyrna, Irenaeus heard a sound in the city of Rome like a trumpet blowing saying, "Polycarp has been martyred." (5) As has been said, Gaius transcribed this story from the writings of Irenaeus and Isocrates took it from the writings of Gaius in Corinth. And I, Pionius, taking it from the writings of Isocrates according to the revelation given me by Polycarp, sought them out and gathered them from writings that were nearly worn out from age so that the Lord Jesus may also gather me with his elect into the heavenly kingdom. To whom be glory with the Father, and the Son, and the Holy Spirit forever and ever. Amen.

---

43 The Greek verb *epiginosko* has the same range of meaning as the English word "recognize." Recognize can mean "notice by remembering" or "give approval." Polycarp is drawing on this double meaning to rebuke Marcion.

Bibliography

Battifol, Pierre. *L'Eucharistie: La Présence Réele et la Transubstantiation* 5th ed. (Paris: Libraire Victor Lecoffre, 1913).

Bauer, Walter, William Arndt, and F. Wilbur Gingerich. *A Lexicon of the New Testament and Other Early Christian Literature* (Chicago: University of Chicago Press, 1952).

Bauer, Walter and Henning Paulsen. *Die Briefe des Ignatius von Antiochia und der Polykarpbrief* in *Handbuch zum Neuen Testament*, vol. 18 (Tubingen: J.C.B. Mohr (Paul Siebeck), 1985).

Bauer, Walter. *Orthodoxy and Heresy in Earliest Christianity* (Philadelphia: Fortress Press, 1971).

Berding, Kenneth. *Polycarp and Paul An Analysis of their Literary & Theological Relationship in light of Polycarp's Use of Biblical and Extra-Biblical Literature* (Leiden: Brill, 2002).

Bihlmeyer K. and W. Schneemelcher (post F.X. Funk). *Die apostolischen Väter*, 3rd ed. (Tübingen: Mohr, 1970).

Bultmann, Rudolf. "Ignatius and Paul" in *Existence and Faith The Shorter Writings of Rudolf Bultmann* Schubert Ogden, editor and translator (New York: The World Publishing Company, 1960) pp. 267-277.

Camelot, P.Th. *Ignace d'Antioche. Polycarpe de Smyrne. Lettres. Martyre de Polycarpe*, 4th ed. *Sources chrétiennes* 10. (Paris: Éditions du Cerf, 1969).

Chrysostom, John. *Encomion on the Holy Martyr Ignatius, Theophorus, Archbishop of Antioch the Great conducted to Rome and there martyred and from there again laid to rest to Antioch* found on the online *Thesaurus Linguae Graecae*.

Ehrman, Bart. (editor and translator) *The Apostolic Fathers* (Cambridge, MA: Harvard University Press, 2003).

Grant, Robert M. *The Apostolic Fathers: a New Translation and Commentary* vol. 1 *An Introduction* (New York: Thomas Nelson and Sons, 1964).

Holmes, Michael W. (editor and translator) *The Apostolic Fathers Greek Texts and English Translations* 3rd ed. (Grand Rapids: Baker Academic, 2007) first published 1992.

Kleist, James S.J. *The Epistles of Clement of Rome and St. Ignatius of Antioch* (Westminster, MD: The Newman Press, 1961).

Lampe, G.W.H. (ed) *A Greek Patristic Lexicon* (Oxford: Oxford University Press, 1961).

Lighfoot, Joseph B. *The Apostolic Fathers: Clement, Ignatius, Polycarp* vols. 1 and 2. Original published by MacMillan in 1889 (Peabody, MA: Hendrickson reprint, 1989).

Musurillo, H. *The acts of the Christian martyrs.* (Oxford: Clarendon Press, 1972).

Ramsey, Boniface. *Beginning to Read the Fathers* (New York: Paulist Press, 1985).

Schoedel, William R. *Ignatius of Antioch Hermeneia Series – A Critical and Historical Commentary on the Bible* (Philadelphia: Fortress Press, 1985).

Schoedel, William R. "Polycarp of Smyrna and Ignatius of Antioch" in Aufstieg und Niedergang der Römischen Welt vol. 27 part 1 (1993) pp. 272-358.

Index of Principal Greek Terms

Explanation: only the most important Greek words mentioned in the book are listed here. The reader should keep in mind that the translations given below are only indicators of the general meaning. In some contexts, these words can be translated with different English words. Since Greek verbs can have many inflected forms, I have listed them below as they usually appear in dictionaries (lexicons) of ancient Greek.

presbuteros (presbyter, elder) 25
presbuterion (presbytery) 76
prokathemai (preside) 45
prosopolempsia (distinction of persons) 152

romaios (Roman) 44, 112

schisma (schism) 79
schoinion (rope) 21
scholazo (be at leisure) 140, 144
sophroneo (think soberly) 151
summustai (fellow initiates) 84
sundoulos (fellow servant) 4, 76
suntrecho (run with, agree with) 77
sussemon (banner, battle standard) 130

tagma (order) 115
telos (purpose, goal) 29, 94
theriomacheo (battle with beasts) 75
therion (beast) 132
thusia (sacrifice) 169
thusiasterion (altar) 79
tupos (type, exemplar) 104

Index

Note: Page numbers followed by an "n" and a number refer to the specified note on the designated page.

About the Author

Kenneth J. Howell is Director and Senior Fellow of the *St. John Institute of Catholic Thought* that is located on the campus of the University of Illinois, Urbana-Champaign. He is also Adjunct Associate Professor in the Department of Religion of the University of Illinois where he teaches classes on the history, theology, and philosophy of Catholicism. He has been a visiting professor at several universities, including the University of Sacramento, and has been a guest lecturer at the universities of Notre Dame, Saint Thomas, and Iowa State on the history of science and religion. He is the author of eight books, including a major study of Copernican cosmology and biblical interpretation in the Scientific Revolution. He has also published dozens of articles in scholarly and popular journals. His current research involves ancient pagan and Christian authors (Clement of Rome, John Chrysostom, Peter Chrysologus, Epicureans, Stoics). He also acts as a theological advisor for *The Coming Home Network International.*

Acknowledgements

I wish to express my appreciation for those who have made the publication of this book possible. My editors, David Hazen and Marie Jutras, have made invaluable suggestions. Mary Clare Piecynski has worked tirelessly on the internal editing and lay-out of the book while Jennifer Bitler designed the cover. Louise Toft prepared the general index. Ann Moore and Robert Rodgers have facilitated the publication process. Most especially, I would like to thank Marcus Grodi for the original inspiration to translate and comment on St. Ignatius and St. Polycarp.

Additional titles by Dr. Kenneth J. Howell

❖Mary of Nazareth
❖Meeting Mary Learning Guide: Our Mother in Faith
❖Why Mary?
❖The Hidden Jesus
❖The Eucharist for Beginners: Sacrament, Sacrifice and Communion
❖God's Two Books: Copernican Cosmology and Biblical Interpretation in Early Modern Science
❖The Teaching of Christ on Priestly Celibacy

Also available from CHResources

Journeys Home Revised Edition......................$12.95
Edited by Marcus Grodi #2522

This book is the foundation of what the *Coming Home Network* is all about: the journeys of Protestant clergy and laity coming home to the Catholic Church. This book contains the stories of many prominent clergy converts.

How Firm A Foundation................................$14.95
By Marcus Grodi #2582

Stephen LaPointe is a minister who loves Jesus, loves to preach, and considers the Bible as the one sufficient, firm foundation for his life. He knows that one day he will stand before God accountable for what he preaches, and it is in this conviction that his crisis begins, for how can he know for certain that what he preaches is eternally true?

Christ in His Fullness..................................$12.95
By Bruce Sullivan #3083

Christ in His Fullness deals with the many reasons for becoming Catholic. Bruce Sullivan lays out an informative study of many of the issues that keep many from ever considering the Catholic Church.

Roots of the Reformation......................................$5.95
By Karl Adam #2523

Karl Adam gives an historically sensitive and accurate analysis of the causes of the Reformation that stands as a valid and sometimes unsettling challenge to the presuppositions of Protestants and Catholics alike. *Roots of the Reformation* is a powerful summary of the issues that led to the Reformation and their implications today.

Catholic Doctrine in Scripture..........................$5.95
By Gregory Oatis #3009

Catholic Doctrine in Scripture is a compendium of Scripture verses, topically arranged and easy to use, which illustrate the scriptural affirmation of Catholic teachings.

Read the Bible and the Catechism in a Year..............$0.50
#5003
This pamphlet provides an excellent daily system for reading the entire Bible and Catechism together in one year!

Tabs for the Catechism of the Catholic Church..........$4.00
#5001

Tabs for the 2nd edition *Catechism of the Catholic Church.* These handy tabs give quick and easy reference of the teachings of the Church on 25 topics and include a subject index. Easily find any topic.

A Scriptural Novena to the Holy Name of our Lord Jesus Christ...$1.95
3122
This Novena prayer consists of a series of fifteen Scripture readings focused on devotion to the Name of Jesus.

Steps To Happiness..$1.95
3123
A brief guide that summarizes step by step how by grace we can attain to true happiness through Jesus Christ and His Body, the Church.

To order please call 1-800-664-5110 or visit
www.chresources.com

Notes

Notes

Notes

Notes